Editor: Rick Joyner
Contributing Editors: Jack Deere, Francis Frangipane, Dudley Hall
Managing Editor: Deborah Joyner Johnson
Project Manager: Dana Zondory
Layout and Design: Dana Zondory
Copy Editors: Suzanne Hirt, Tracey Selvey, and Deborah Williams

The Morning Star Journal® USPS012-903 is published quarterly, 4 issues per year, by MorningStar Publications, Inc. A division of MorningStar Fellowship Church, P.O. Box 440, Wilkesboro, NC 28697. Fall 2005 issue. Periodicals postage rates paid at North Wilkesboro, NC and additional mailing offices. CPC Agreement #1472593. ISSN# 10832122

POSTMASTER: Send address corrections to *The Morning Star Journal*®, P.O. Box 440, Wilkesboro, NC 28697

Subscription rates: One year $16.95; Outside U.S. $24.95 USD.

MorningStar Publications is a non-profit organization dedicated to the promulgation of important teachings and timely prophetic messages to the church. We also attempt to promote interchange between the different streams and denominations in the body of Christ.

To receive a subscription to *The Morning Star Journal*®, send payment along with your name and address to *MorningStar Publications*, P.O. Box 440, Wilkesboro, NC 28697, (336) 651-2400 (1-800-542-0278—Credit Card Orders Only); fax (336) 651-2430. One year (4 quarterly issues) U.S. $16.95; Outside U.S. $24.95 USD. Prices are subject to change without notice.

Reprints—Photocopies of any part of the contents of this publication may be made freely. However, to re-typeset information, permission must be requested in writing from *MorningStar Publications Department*, P.O. Box 440, Wilkesboro, NC 28697

BIOS

Francis Frangipane is the senior pastor of River of Life Ministries in Cedar Rapids, Iowa, and the president of Advancing Church Ministries. The Lord has used Francis to unite thousands of pastors in prayer in hundreds of cities. With more than a million copies of his best-selling books in print, and with an expanding radio and television ministry called "In Christ's Image," Francis is in much demand worldwide. His newest book is entitled, *This Day We Fight!*

Mike Roberts is originally from the Charlotte, North Carolina area and has been involved at MorningStar for about ten years. He is a graduate of the MorningStar School of Ministry, and has a heart for the prophetic ministry and teaching. Mike is currently on staff at MorningStar Publications and Ministries and lives in Moravian Falls, North Carolina.

Hombre Liggett is ordained through MorningStar Fellowship of Ministries and is the founding pastor of Church of the Harvest, located in Dover, Ohio. Hombre's heart is to lead the members of the body of Christ into prophetic worship, equipped to fulfill their purpose, and provide a platform for them to function. The foundation of his twelve-year ministry is the love of God and the unity of the Spirit.

Dan Duke has thirty-four years of ministry experience in approximately fifty nations. He and his wife of thirty-five years, Marti, currently reside in Belo Horizonte, Brazil from where they travel extensively throughout the nation. Dan graduated with a Doctor of Theology degree from the Jacksonville Theological Seminary and is the author of several books including: *Apostolic Ministry, The Impartation, Messages for the Revival Generation,* and *The Encyclopedia of Proper Names and Numbers of the Bible.* Dan and Marti have four children and seven grandchildren.

Deborah Joyner Johnson is the managing editor for MorningStar Publications and Ministries. She shares with her brother, Rick Joyner, a desire to see the body of Christ provided with the highest quality spiritual food that is relevant for our times. Deborah's second book, *Pathway to Purpose,* was recently released through MorningStar. She has a gifted teaching ministry and shares at conferences and women's groups. Deborah lives in North Carolina and has three children: Matthew, Meredith, and Abby.

BIOS

Steve Thompson is the associate director of MorningStar Fellowship Church, and he oversees the prophetic ministries for all of the MorningStar Fellowships. A gifted teacher and prophetic minister, Steve travels extensively throughout the United States and abroad as a conference speaker. Steve's newest book, *A 20ᵗʰ Century Apostle, The Life of Alfred Garr,* was released through MorningStar. Steve and his wife, Angie, reside in North Carolina with their five children: Jon, Josh, Madison, Moriah, and Olivia.

Trevor Tiessen is originally from Saskatchewan, Canada. In the fall of 1996 Trevor came to Charlotte, North Carolina to attend the MorningStar School of Ministry and graduated in the spring of 1999. Since that time Trevor has been serving MorningStar Fellowship Church in the areas of church and conference administration as well as in the ministry of helps.

Robin McMillan is currently the pastor of MorningStar Fellowship Church at our H.I.M. facilities near Charlotte, North Carolina. With a unique preaching style, prophetic giftings, and a desire for the release of God's power, many are impacted by Robin's ministry. Robin and his wife, Donna, live in North Carolina and have four children: John Mark, Christopher, Andy, and Katy.

Paul Goulet is the senior pastor of the International Church of Las Vegas. Since he came to Las Vegas in 1992, the church has grown from 270 attendants to over four thousand. He has a vision to start two thousand churches by the year 2020. Pastor Goulet travels extensively sharing his life-transforming messages at conferences, crusades and churches all over the world. He has written many books, including *The Breakthrough Series, Jesus I want to know Him, The Power of Impartation, The Power of Impartation in the Home, The Five Powers,* and *The Threshold.*

John Paul Jackson is the founder and chairman of Streams Ministries International located in North Sutton, New Hampshire. A popular teacher and conference speaker, John Paul travels around the world teaching on prophetic gifts, dreams, visions, and the realm of the supernatural. His newest publication, *Moments With God Dream Journal,* offers a unique approach to dream recording. To order his books and tapes, please call 1-888-441-8080, or visit his website at www.streamsministries.com.

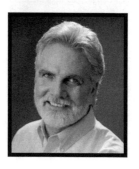

BIOS

Rick Joyner is the founder, executive director, and senior pastor of MorningStar Fellowship Church. Rick is a well-known author of more than thirty books, including, *The Torch and the Sword*, the long awaited sequel to *The Final Quest* and *The Call*, and his latest, *Delivered From Evil*. He also oversees MorningStar's School of Ministry, Fellowship of Ministries, and Fellowship of Churches. Rick and his wife, Julie, live in North Carolina with their five children: Anna, Aaryn, Amber, Ben, and Sam.

Sally Boenau is an MFM and MST member who is actively involved in the prayer ministries of her church and community. Sally has recently founded "Spirit and Life Lighters" which distributes marketplace friendly products such as seed packets, magnets, and soaps with messages based on the words of Jesus. To learn more about Sally's products, email her at: bripatch@brinet.com. Sally and her husband, Doug, have been married for forty-two years and have one daughter and two grandchildren. They live in Hendersonville, North Carolina.

Paul Keith Davis and his wife, Wanda, are founders of WhiteDove Ministries. They travel extensively imparting the end-time mandate of preparation for the glory and manifest presence of Christ. He and Bob Jones write *The Shepherd's Rod*, yearly. Paul Keith has also written the book, *The Thrones of Our Soul*. He and his wife reside in Alabama. Together they have five children and three grandchildren.

Colin Brown oversees Shiloh Fellowship, a ministry and church in Australia, based in Ulverstone on Tasmania's northwest coast. With his wife Tina, and two of his four children, they spent eighteen months with DaySpring Christian Fellowship in Sydney through the end of 2004. An important aspect of the ministry of Shiloh Fellowship is Colin's writing, in order to bring timely encouragement and insight, especially in the face of these exciting yet sobering times. You may email him at: www.shilohfellowship.org.au.

The MEASURE of MATURITY

by Francis Frangipane

It has been my experience that too many of us, as Christians, have been confused about love. We have assumed that attaining the look of love is the same reality as actually being transformed into a loving person. I am not saying that we have consciously planned on being shallow or noncommittal, but that somehow we have settled on the cosmetic instead of the real.

We have developed an "altar" ego, a look for church that lasts at best just a few minutes longer than the church service itself. All we have really accomplished is to perfect the art of acting like Christians. I think we have yet to learn to consistently walk according to the standards of Christ's love. I hear how quick some are to speak about the flaws of those they supposedly love, and I wonder what kind of love demeans individuals behind their backs? When I witness unloving words from a Christian's mouth, I am reminded that we have much to learn about Jesus and what it means to follow Him.

David prayed, **"Let the words of my mouth and the meditation of my heart be acceptable in Thy sight, O LORD, my rock and my Redeemer" (Psalm 19:14).**

Our words are the by-product of our meditations. Whatever is brooding in our hearts will eventually ascend to our lips. If we have unforgiveness prowling within, our conversations will be barbed with negative comments—even in moments of lighthearted banter. If we are harboring bitterness, it will slice through our speech. Jesus taught that **"the mouth speaks out of that which fills the heart" (Matthew 12:34).** We cannot fix our words without first fixing our hearts. attatads + Tunis.

When the Lord judges us for our words, it is because He is seeking to purify our hearts. True, the heart is deceitful above all things and it is difficult to know our own iniquity. Yet if we simply pause and listen to how many of our words are without love, we can track them back to the real problem: loveless hearts.

A New Anointing

Christians are in the fire of God. The Holy Spirit is purging the church from negative chatter. A fresh anointing is at hand where God's people shall speak with the character necessary to represent Him. What the Lord told the prophet Jeremiah, He is speaking also to us:

> Therefore, thus says the LORD, "If you return, then I will restore you—before Me you will stand; and if you extract the precious from the worthless, you will become My spokesman" (Jeremiah 15:19).

Let us pray that as God exposes our lack of love that a time will soon come when we will pray with credibility: "You have tried my heart; You have visited me by night; You have tested me and You find nothing; I have purposed that my mouth will not transgress" (Psalm 17:3).

Do we see this? God judges the quality of our entire lives by the soundness and substance of our words. Thus Jesus warned, "But I tell you that every careless word that people speak, they shall give an accounting for it in the day of judgment" (Matthew 12:36). Let us consider Christ's warning soberly. He continued, "For by your words you will be justified, and by your words you will be condemned" (Matthew 12:37 NKJV). James adds, "judgment will be merciless to one who has shown no mercy; mercy triumphs over judgment" (James 2:13). I have a holy fear in my heart concerning these warnings. I know if I am merciless toward others, God will be merciless toward me.

Character Counts

Sometimes I think we try to mask our critical attitude by calling it "discernment." The fact is, most of what manifests in our discussions about others is simply judging after the flesh. If we truly love individuals, we will be as loving in their absence as we are in their presence.

Jesus said His disciples would be known by their love (see John 13:35). Paul said that the love of Christ is supposed to control us (see II Corinthians 5:14), which means it is the nature and discipline of love that keeps us from joining in verbal attacks or even subtle criticisms. You see, it takes character to avoid being sucked into gossip and criticisms. There is a high road we can take. It starts with prayer; it extends to grace; it is slow to speak; it approaches an individual with a meek heart; it talks privately with the person; it is forgiving when wronged and patient with the spiritually immature.

Of course, if someone is involved with criminal activity or seriously endangering others through his sin, we must love the greater community and take steps to protect the innocent. There is a time to discipline or even publicly expose sin (see Matthew 18:15-17), but it is after we exhaust other means of correction—and even then, our motive should communicate our hope of redemption and not allow our disclosure to become a smokescreen for revenge. In all things, love must guide our words.

> "WHEN SOMEONE LOVES YOU, THE WAY THEY SAY YOUR NAME IS DIFFERENT. YOU JUST KNOW THAT YOUR NAME IS SAFE IN THEIR MOUTH."

Child's Eye View of Love

Recently my youngest daughter, Eden, sent me a list of quotes that came from little children. Each child was asked to describe what love meant to them. Their answers were, at times, quite intriguing. One in particular, from a four year old boy named Billy, has stuck with me. He said, "When someone loves you, the way they say your name is different. You just know that your name is safe in their mouth."

That thought seems to say it all: "When someone loves you…your name is safe in their mouth." Behold this clarity of vision as love is defined by a little child. When we truly walk in Christ's love, those around us will be safe, and others will see the love of Christ that controls us.

Beloved, to walk in covering love is to show ourselves truly acquainted with Christ. Let us ask God, "Father, show me my heart. Is Your love ruling, even in the unseen areas of my life? Are the names of others safe in my mouth?" ∎

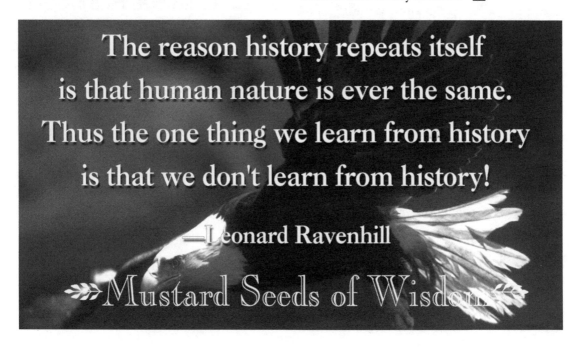

The reason history repeats itself is that human nature is ever the same. Thus the one thing we learn from history is that we don't learn from history!

—Leonard Ravenhill

Mustard Seeds of Wisdom

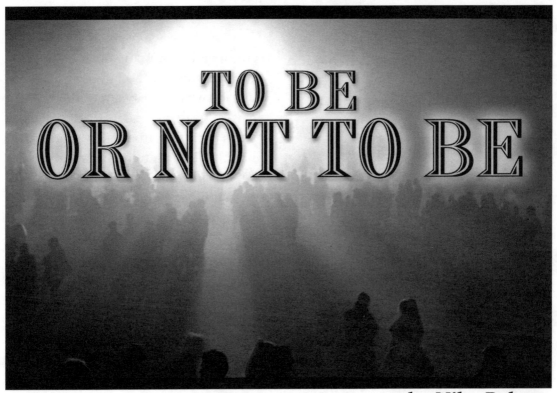

TO BE OR NOT TO BE

by Mike Roberts

Have you ever considered what makes a person great? If you were asked to make a list of people who achieved greatness, who would come to mind? Most people would probably think of Winston Churchill, Abraham Lincoln, Mother Teresa, Michael Jordan, or some other monumental figure. Businessmen would probably make mention of Warren Buffet, Bill Gates, or Jack Welch, and as Christians, we would certainly add Billy Graham, Queen Esther, the apostle Paul, and Corrie Ten Boom to the list.

Let us briefly consider some of these remarkable people. Winston Churchill has been nearly immortalized in the pages of history because he helped lead one of the greatest marches in the preservation of freedom the world has ever known. Michael Jordan is known all over the world for his accomplishments as an athlete; Mother Teresa will forever be remembered for her life of sacrifice and genuine compassion for the poor and needy; Billy Graham is perhaps the most respected man in recent history, and he is especially endeared in the hearts of Christians for uncompromising integrity in his life and ministry as he has shared the gospel of our Lord to literally millions of people.

As we consider these extraordinary people, what did they do that made them great? What ingredients did they have in their lives that others seemed to be missing? How did they rise to the top of their generations?

What are the Key Ingredients?

All of these people, and others like them, probably have several things in common. However, being from a privileged background, having wealth, or getting all the good breaks and opportunities is not a common thread. So what brought them the success they experienced?

Although an extensive study of several remarkable people might produce a long list of common characteristics, the purpose of this article is to examine two of the most important: personal habits and close relationships. A person's habits and the people with whom he associates the most closely will be major determining factors in the quality of his life and accomplishments.

A Matter of Habit

There are few components in a person's daily life that are as instrumental in determining his level of accomplishment as his personal habits. Whether a person accomplishes great things or lives his life at a level far below his potential, his habits will be largely responsible.

Our habits will either work for us or they will work against us. They are completely within our ability to control, and if we control them, they will be some of our greatest assets. However, if we allow them to control us, they will prove to be some of our greatest liabilities.

At first thought, this subject may not seem very spiritual, but the Bible has a great deal to say about our personal habits. They affect nearly every area of our lives: our jobs, our personal relationships, and even the way we think. Our habits are very important to the Lord and our walk with Him will be enhanced or hindered by our habits. Let us examine just a few of the practical ways our habits affect our lives.

Whatever Works

Most of us spend a great deal of time working at our jobs, and work is a part of God's purpose for us. Even before the Fall, God instructed Adam to cultivate and keep the Garden (see Genesis 2:15). Work is fundamentally a part of our calling and purpose, but occasionally a "new idea" surfaces that guarantees quick success without hard work. These ideas have robbed many people, including Christians, of lasting fruit in their lives. The Bible says that:

The plans of the diligent lead surely to advantage, but everyone who is hasty comes surely to poverty (Proverbs 21:5).

He who tills his land will have plenty of food, but he who follows empty pursuits will have poverty in plenty (Proverbs 28:19).

We can be sure that any method which claims to lead to instant success, but does not involve diligence and hard work, will lead only to shallow, short-lived achievements. If we are going to be successful and produce results that are truly lasting, it will be because we have been diligent in cultivating good work habits.

Reach Out and Touch Someone

God has made us relational creatures. We will never be the people God has purposed us to be without each other, and our habits can have a direct effect on the quality of our relationships. For example, let us consider how habits of communication can affect a married couple.

> ...every relationship we have will be helped or hurt by our habits, and we can decide which it will be.

At the beginning of a marriage, probably few things consume the heart of each partner as much as thoughts of the other person. They can sit and talk for hours at a time, staring deeply into one another's eyes, and it only seems to be a few minutes. However, less than a year later, they rarely resemble the same couple they were just a short time ago. Now they are impatient with each other; the husband may not call home to let his wife know that he will be missing dinner, and they often do not take the time to talk and make decisions together.

Although there are many factors that can cause this digression in a relationship, one common reason is that bad habits have developed over time and gone unchecked. The opposite is also true.

When a couple has been together for a long time, and they still glow with the same love and respect for each other, it is largely because they have taken the time to cultivate good habits of communication, forgiveness, and understanding.

It is the same with all relationships. Whether it is parents and children, teachers and students, brothers and sisters, or pastors and church members, every relationship we have will be helped or hurt by our habits, and we can decide which it will be.

You Are What You Think

One of the most common, but over-looked, areas where our habits have a major effect in our lives is in our thoughts. The Bible teaches that the thoughts we consistently think will help determine who we are (see Proverbs 23:7). We have the ability to decide what our thoughts will be. The apostle Paul understood this, as he said in Philippians 4:8:

> **Finally, brethren, whatever is true, whatever is honorable, whatever is right, whatever is pure, whatever is lovely, whatever is of good repute, if there is any excellence and if anything worthy of praise, let your mind dwell on these things.**

If our thoughts are mostly negative, we will be negative people much of the time. If we tend to focus on the problems we face instead of trusting the Lord for the solutions, we will tend to constantly move from one defeat to another. In this life we can be assured that we are going to have to deal with difficult situations, and at times, difficult people. We cannot always control what happens to us, but we are responsible for the way we respond. Defeat in any situation in life often begins with a defeat in our mentality.

However, if our thoughts are positive, this will also be reflected in our lives. If we develop a mentality of being solution oriented, obstacles and unfortunate situations will never be able to stop us, but we will come through them victorious. We will become more than conquerors who are constantly experiencing victory (see II Corinthians 2:14 and Romans 8:37).

The Importance of Relationships

Like our habits, our personal relationships really can "make us or break us." Just like our thoughts, our relationships will play a huge role in determining who we are and what we do. Have you ever heard any of these adages: "You are known by the company you keep," "Lie down with dogs and you will wake up with fleas," or "Birds of a feather flock together?" These are just a few of the many witty, but true, observations that most likely originated with someone who learned this principle the hard way.

The Bible also has much to say about this subject. In I Corinthians 15:33 the apostle Paul said:

Do not be deceived: "Bad company corrupts good morals."

King Solomon also understood this, as he said:

The righteous should choose his friends carefully, for the way of the wicked leads them astray (Proverbs 12:26 NKJV).

He who walks with wise men will be wise, but the companion of fools will be destroyed (Proverbs 13:20 NKJV).

If an aspiring athlete spends time around other athletes who are committed to excelling in their sport, he or she will go much further than they ever would by spending most of their time with people who are content to be mediocre. A young businessman who is mentored by positive, hard-working influences, is more likely to experience long-term success in his career. If our closest relationships are with people who are godly and who have our best interests at heart, they will constantly call us higher and closer to the Lord.

> **Just like our thoughts, our relationships will play a huge role in determining who we are and what we do.**

However, this same principle works the other way. Many a fine young lady has been persuaded to compromise her convictions by giving in to the pressures of friends who did not share her standards. A young man can grow up in a Christian home and then fall into the wrong company in college and, consequently, find himself on a track that will lead to regret ten years later. Whether our closest associates are positive or negative, we will become like these people. This is obviously pertinent for young people, but our friends' ability to influence us never ends with age—that's why it is so important for our close relationships to be good ones.

> **Let us determine to never settle for being less than the very best God has purposed for us to be.**

Just like our habits, our relationships will have a direct effect on our level of achievement. Anyone who has ever achieved greatness and true success surrounded themselves with people who were good influences. Let us determine to do the same.

Conclusion

This article obviously only begins to scratch the surface of these important subjects, but it is helpful to understand the value of our habits and relationships. It is also important to understand that we can determine how they affect our lives, whether negatively or positively. In Matthew 22:14, Jesus made this observation: **"For many are called, but few are chosen."**

He was not saying that it had to be that way, but He said that it commonly was that way. Everyone has potential, but few ever pay the price to walk in the fullness of it. Jesus also talked about a master who gave three of his servants a certain number of talents. The first two people used their talents and actually doubled what their master initially gave them. The third person buried his talents in the ground and never used them (see Matthew 25:14-30).

God has given everyone talents and abilities, and like the first two people in Jesus' parable, some people put their talents to good use. They experience life at a level the ones who bury their talents will never know. Which do we want to be? Do we want to bury our potential in the ground of bad habits and negative relationships or do we want to cultivate these fertile fields to help us produce a bountiful crop with the seeds God has given us? Let us determine to never settle for being less than the very best God has purposed for us to be. Let us consistently surround ourselves with positive influences and discipline our habits so that they work for us, not against us. Taking these two steps can help propel us into a life of greatness and **"an abundance for every good deed" (II Corinthians 9:8).** ∎

No Man Can See Me and Live

by Hombre Liggett

"**B**ut He said, 'You cannot see My face, for no man can see Me and live!'" (Exodus 33:20). Throughout Old Testament history it was understood that if a person encountered the manifest presence of God and saw His face, then he would die. The Lord wants us to clearly know the consequences of getting close to Him and seeing His face, which is death. With that knowledge, He then wants us to choose to pursue a close relationship with Him and see His face!

Seeing God's face is like looking into a spiritual mirror. To see God is to clearly see oneself. Many feel this experience would be an easy one, but in the light of God's perfect holiness, righteousness, and power, our own imperfections are magnified. The state of our hearts and lives become clear in His presence.

In the year of King Uzziah's death, I saw the Lord sitting on a throne, lofty and exalted, with the train of His robe filling the temple.

Then I said, "Woe is me, for I am ruined! Because I am a man of unclean lips, and I live among a people of unclean lips; for my eyes have seen the King, the LORD of hosts." (Isaiah 6:1,5).

Even though Isaiah was a seasoned prophet, when he came face to face with God he said, **"Woe is me, for I am ruined!"** God's presence displays an awesome power, which is the most extreme threat to our natural way of living. The day the Lord appears to us is a great and terrible moment for our flesh and carnal lifestyles. His presence leaves no hope for carnality and brings certain doom to remaining as we were before the experience.

When Moses got a glimpse of the Living God, the Bible says **"so terrible was the sight, that Moses said, 'I am full of fear and trembling'" (Hebrews 12:21).**

God first made it clear that if anyone sees His face they will die, but as stated, He also intentionally encourages us to seek after His face.

> **EVERY TIME I GET A GLIMPSE OF HIM, A LITTLE MORE OF MY LIFE DIES, AND MORE OF HIS LIFE COMES ALIVE IN ME.**

And (*if*) My people who are called by My name humble themselves and pray, and *seek My face* and turn from their wicked ways, then I will hear from heaven, will forgive their sin, and will heal their land (II Chronicles 7:14, emphasis mine).

Seek the Lord and His strength; seek His face continually (I Chronicles 16:11).

If we seek and see His face, then won't we die? Yes! That is the point. Death is the goal. God desires to bring death to

our old nature, or more specifically, God desires to kill the natural in us that we might live in the supernatural.

For God to intimately hear us, forgive us, and bring healing to that depth in our lives, we must humbly seek His face...and die. This reality is continued in the New Testament.

And He was saying to them all, "If anyone wishes to come after Me, he must deny himself, and take up his cross daily, and follow Me.

For whoever wishes to save his life will lose it, but whoever loses his life for My sake, he is the one who will save it" (Luke 9:23-24).

I have had experiences where I have found myself in the unique manifest presence of God, and on each occasion I knew that I would never be the same. It is a result of seeking God's face that the most profound heart level changes have been made in my life. Every time I get a glimpse of Him, a little more of my life dies, and more of His life comes alive in me.

When we see God, we then also see ourselves for who we are. We see our hearts compared to Him, and in that moment we know that things about us must die. In this experience it becomes clear that the level of changes needed to be made in our lives could never be done on our own. It appears that Isaiah may have been thinking something like this when he saw the Lord, "How can I continue? I am unclean to the point to which I could never remedy! Who am I compared to such awesome holiness and power? There is no way to go on! I am ruined!"

Yet, it was also in that moment that God prepared Isaiah for the greater part of his ministry on the earth. It is an oxymoron to say we want to experience God's presence, but at the same time not be willing to be personally changed. It is a dilemma for many Christians. Some say they want to change, and yet they do not seek God's face. Others say they want to see God's face, but fight any real change in their lives.

We can only truly be changed in God's presence. We must not make the mistake of trying to develop our lives into a condition that we feel is worthy of approaching God. There is no such condition. He is God, and there is none like Him who could ever compare. We are not to try to change ourselves in order to come into God's presence, but by the blood of Christ we should come into God's presence in order to be changed.

One of the things that made King David so unique and useable by God is that he did not resist the operable hand of the Lord in his life. David knew God's love, and therefore he did not fear the Lord's face. He understood that seeing God meant difficult changes in his life, yet his passion for God caused him to pursue the Lord and allow those changes to be made at any cost.

David was not a perfect man when God called him, nor was David worthy of God's calling. God did not find David the way He needed him. He found him

teachable, breakable, and reformable. David was willing to die and be recreated according to God's design. Listen to what he wrote concerning seeking God's face.

> **When You said, "Seek My face," my heart said to You, "Your face, O LORD, I shall seek" (Psalm 27:8).**

> **Seek the LORD and His strength; seek His face continually (Psalm 105:4).**

> **And He was saying to them all, "If anyone wishes to come after Me, he must deny himself, and take up his cross daily and follow Me" (Luke 9:23).**

WE MUST NOT MAKE THE MISTAKE OF TRYING TO DEVELOP OUR LIVES INTO A CONDITION THAT WE FEEL IS WORTHY OF APPROACHING GOD.

People often try to figure out how to take up the cross of Christ, and like Paul, to die daily. Every day there are practical opportunities to take up our crosses and live for God. Coming to the cross of Christ daily is built upon the foundation of seeking God's face daily. This is by the design of God, and it has always existed for man. By doing this we will both die to things in our lives that are offensive to the Lord and make higher level sacrifices in our service to Him.

Before the Fall, Adam was accustomed to walking with and seeing God every morning in the Garden. Isaiah also developed a comparable relationship with the Lord. He became accustomed to being with God every morning and allowing the Lord to teach and instruct him. Isaiah wrote:

The Lord God has given me the tongue of disciples, that I may know how to sustain the weary one with a word. He awakens me morning by morning, He awakens my ear to listen as a disciple (Isaiah 50:4).

ENTER GOD'S PRESENCE WITH A WILLINGNESS TO EARNESTLY EXPOSE THE IMPURITIES IN YOUR HEART...

Those daily opportunities become aggressively easier to embark upon as a result of spending time seeking the Lord's face. They are less of a burden when we are more dead to self, living in a greater revelation of God and in a closer fellowship with Him.

If we would begin to pursue God in this nature, then the results of such a pursuit would develop in our lives quickly. God draws near to those who draw near to Him, and He rewards those who are seeking after His face.

And without faith it is impossible to please God, because anyone who comes to him must believe that he exists and that he rewards those who earnestly seek him (Hebrew 11:6 NIV).

There are practical ways to seek after the face of God, which speaks of evolving an intimate relationship with Him. We need to meditate upon God's Word (see Psalm 1), be devoted to prayer (see Luke 18:1), and maintain a strong relationship with a fellowship of the body of Christ (see Hebrews 10:24-26). Additionally, God desires to bring extra-biblical like experiences to your relationship with Him. This would include, but not be limited to: angelic visitations, visions, dreams, and most importantly, His manifest presence.

As you seek Him, do not fight the things you begin to see in yourself. Do as King David did. Enter God's presence with a willingness to earnestly expose the impurities in your heart, and then allow God to forgive, change, and heal you. This is a large part of the process of dying daily, and it will help your decisions throughout the day. Your service to God will come easier and with greater anointing.

God is clearly calling us to come seek His face and die to our self-life (the natural life), so that we might grow in the supernatural life of Christ Jesus our Lord. Seek the Lord's face and live! ∎

The Manna Ceased

by Dan Duke

"The manna ceased..." (Joshua 5:12)

That is such a simple statement of fact isn't it? The manna ceased...end of subject.

Well not exactly. The day after they crossed over the Jordan into their Promised Land they ate the old corn of the land. After forty years of doing things in a particular and dependable way, the manna ceased. For the generation born in the wilderness it was all they had ever known and all they had ever eaten or tasted (though they did get quail in response to the whining of their fathers). When they entered their Promised Land, the sweet manna of the wilderness was to be no more.

Without any previous warning, God was now going to do something new and provide for them in a different way. No longer could they wake up a little early before the sun became hot and go outside and gather a basket of manna so breakfast could be prepared.

I suppose those entering the much acclaimed Promised Land were a bit surprised and even a little disappointed. The old corn did not come close to the taste of the sweet manna from heaven that fell fresh every day.

Change and promotion can be, and most of the time is, disguised. For example, when the children of Israel were "delivered" from the bondage of Egypt and journeyed into the wilderness (which incidentally was to be a brief journey), they immediately discovered this "deliverance" was not at all what they thought it was going to be. After all, they carried with them their 430 years of back wages. They were all wealthy and healthy but, alas, there was no water to be found at any price. There was, in fact, nothing to buy at all. The only place to spend their money was on the tabernacle in the wilderness. They were to finance a house for God and a place of worship.

From that moment, the complaining set in. The murmurings in the wilderness replaced the sound of the crack of the Egyptian's whip. "At least we had onions in Egypt," was their pitiful cry.

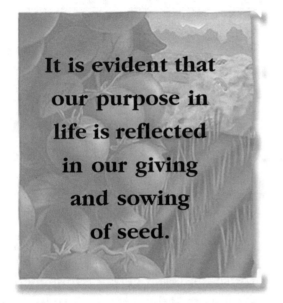

It is evident that our purpose in life is reflected in our giving and sowing of seed.

God's ways are not our ways. The sooner we discover this, the better. The Promised Land was indeed a land of milk and honey. However, God's plan for their provision had changed. Those who resist God's change remain in the wilderness regardless of where they are.

The wilderness generation only knew daily provision. They never had a new pair of shoes in all their life. I suppose those little sandals they had as babies grew as their feet grew. Can you imagine wearing the same pair of shoes for forty years?

God's loving desire was to bring His people from a daily provision of just enough to a much greater measure. In the Promised Land, it was to be from harvest to harvest. The small basket used to gather a day's allotment of manna was to be replaced by barns and threshing floors. The daily limitation was to be thrown out and replaced by a limitless supply of harvest depending on the seed that was sown. In the Promised Land they could determine their own harvest, both in size and description.

Before there was an Israelite nation there was the Word of God recorded in Genesis 8:22, **"While the earth remains, seedtime and harvest, and cold and heat, and summer and winter, and day and night shall not cease."** The plan and purpose of God was to bring the people of Israel into the supernatural provision and kingdom prosperity that sowing and reaping alone can produce. No longer were they to live by a day-to-day existence. It was no longer to be just enough for today and no more, they could determine their harvest by the seed they would sow.

We see this principle carried over into the New Testament with the words of the apostle Paul: **"he who sows sparingly shall also reap sparingly; and he who sows bountifully shall reap bountifully. Let each one do just as he has purposed in his heart, not grudgingly or under compulsion, for God loves a cheerful giver (II Corinthians 9:6-7).**

It is evident that our purpose in life is reflected in our giving and sowing of seed. Those of small purpose, which is an "I, me, mine, enough for today mentality" are, and always will be, small givers. Their harvest will be small because their seed is given sparingly. They, therefore, limit themselves to a small harvest. Religion has so shaped their mentality so to have enough to pay their bills and meet the basic needs of their family and is interpreted as the blessing of God and life in the Promised Land. I remind you that it was in the wilderness they met the basic needs of their family by gathering manna each day.

God had something better for them in the land of promise—if they could only see it. But it came to them in the form of old corn—hardly what they expected. It will profit you greatly to remember that the seed never looks like the fruit. An apple seed looks nothing like an apple. You have to recognize it for what it is—a seed.

I have made the decision as to where I choose to live—the wilderness or the Promised Land. That decision determines how I live and how my provision comes. I have chosen to cross the Jordan and live in my Promised Land so I must accept the way it is...seedtime and harvest is to be my provision. To coin an old phrase, "it comes with the territory." My opinion, likes or dislikes, do not matter. I live by the law of the land or I do without. The law of Genesis says...my harvest comes from my seed. *No seed, no harvest.*

If I want to determine my own level of living, which I do, then I must accept the reality that "with the same measure that I measure [my giving] it shall be measured to me again." My purpose which

is to be a blessing must be reflected, not in word alone, but in action. That is why I have the goal to give something to someone every day of my life. I passed a woman, someone's mother, sitting barefooted in the street today. I gave her some money. She wept. "Now I can have food," she cried. The few bucks I gave her meant nothing to me, but it meant everything to her. We must learn to weep with those who weep.

...I have the goal to give something to someone every day of my life.

There are at least four things that I aspire to do every day. I worship, pray, read my Bible, and give an offering to someone as a seed sown. There are days I fall short of one or more of those things but those days are few. It is my goal to accomplish those four things every day. My life, then, does not reflect my value as a preacher or my value as an employee of an organization. My lifestyle reflects my giving. Literally, I live by giving. In the Promised Land, one moves from a day-to-day living into a harvest-to-harvest living. If you desire a harvest, sow a seed. If you desire a harvest as a lifestyle then giving must become your lifestyle. What could be simpler?

The wisest and the wealthiest man in the Bible, Solomon, gives us this free advice, "Cast your bread on the waters, for you shall find it after many days. Give a portion to seven or eight, for you do not know what evil shall come on the earth...In the morning sow your seed, and in the evening withhold not your hand, for you don't know which shall prosper, either this or that, or whether they both shall be good" (see Ecclesiastes 11:1-6).

> **Do not make the mistake Israel made by becoming, in their own eyes, the object of God's blessing.**

Again, Solomon, our financial counselor and wise mentor says, **"The liberal soul shall be made fat; and he that watereth** [others] **shall be watered also himself."** The Portuguese Bible translates the verse this way: **"The generous soul shall become prosperous" (Proverbs 11:25 KJV).** Do you believe it?

When I die I want to leave behind the legacy of being a generous man. I would like for my friends and family to say of me, "Dan was the most generous person I have ever known." In order for that to be a reality I must live in the Promised Land. I must always have a harvest sufficient for what I need for my immediate family and for my greater spiritual family. To give is my life and my joy. I pray it can be yours as well.

"Be a giver. Be a generous person. Look for people and projects to give to and seek to be a channel of provision to as many people as possible." God made a promise to Abraham that in his seed all the nations of the world would be blessed (see Genesis 22:18). That promise was directly fulfilled in Jesus, the Promised Deed. However, you who are of faith are also the seed of Abraham our father in the faith.

Do not make the mistake Israel made by becoming, in their own eyes, the object of God's blessing. They were to be the channel of God's blessing, not the object. When you become the object, the blessing stops. When you are only the channel of God's blessing flowing out to others, the well will never dry up, the meal barrel will never become empty, and the oil will never stop flowing. ■

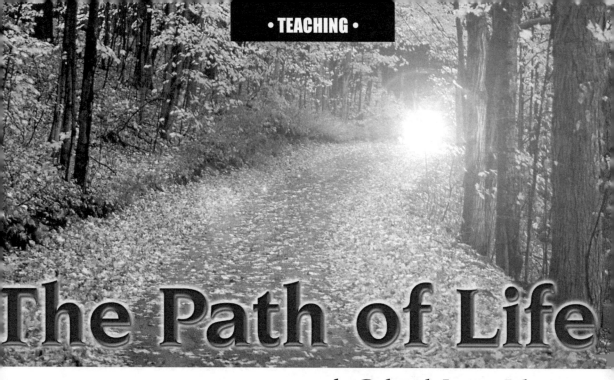

The Path of Life

by Deborah Joyner Johnson

Following the path of life will lead us to an extraordinary life filled with purpose. More importantly, this path will lead us to a closer walk with the Lord.

At times, however, the path may seem very narrow and hard to see. Our vision may become clouded as discouragement or even the temptation of sin seeks to sway us off the path of life. All around us the enemy is looking for ways to entice us to walk onto his path—an imitation of what God intends for our lives, a path of destruction. Many have fallen prey to the enemy's traps, but with wisdom and the Lord's guidance we can walk past his snares, never suffering from the consequences to which he would have us fall. And then, we can savor the sweetest kind of victory, knowing we have pleased the Lord by being true to Him.

Jesus, Our Guide

When Jesus called Peter and Andrew to be His disciples, He said: **"Follow Me"** (see Matthew 4:19). From that day of decision to follow Him, they began an empowering relationship with Jesus that changed their lives forever. Jesus taught, guided, rebuked, healed, nourished them, and became their Friend. Peter, Andrew, and the rest of His disciples led tremendously rewarding lives, developing a close relationship with Jesus because they chose to follow and spend time with Him.

Jesus is simply saying to us: **"Follow Me,"** so we can do the same. As we follow the Lord and learn of His ways and wisdom, He will become the perfect Guide, steering us away from the enemy's trap, and onto the path He desires for us to follow. We will then experience the most rewarding life ever imaginable as we become closer to Him.

Soon after Jesus died and rose again, He commissioned His disciples to teach others about Him. As He was departing to be with His Father, He gave this promise: **"Lo, I am with you always, even to the end of the age" (Matthew 28:20).** The disciples did what Jesus asked and taught others about Him. In so doing, their relationships with Him continued to deepen even down a most difficult path upon which they were asked to walk. They held onto His promise that He would always be with them. Their love for Him became so great that it did not matter what others thought, that they were persecuted, and even that they died horrible deaths. To proclaim that Jesus was Lord was worth it all! Nothing stopped them from following Him.

Similarly, we are to teach others about Him, that they may come to know the Lord. We must be sure to inform them when they begin their walks with Him that the path ahead will not be easy. But if they will be faithful to follow the Lord wherever He leads, clinging to the promise that He will always be with them, they will live the most amazing and rewarding lives possible.

The Shepherd's Voice

In John 10:27-28, Jesus said: **"My sheep hear My voice, and I know them, and they follow Me; and I give eternal life to them, and they shall never perish; and no one shall snatch them out of My hand."** We all know the voice of our closest friends. Likewise, the secret to following Jesus is to know His voice—that we might hear His counsel.

We have the opportunity to set our vision toward Him and follow Him, knowing that He will not lead us astray. The only time we can be led astray is when we take our vision off of Him so that we no longer hear His voice. We have an enemy who is trying to stop us at every turn. Do not give him a chance. With the Lord's guidance, we can thwart the enemy's plans and finish the courses the Lord has set before us.

The Greatest Pleasure of All

We would never intentionally hurt those we love. Sometimes I think about how much it must hurt the Lord to see His children going astray. If you have ever experienced your own child or a close friend falling into sin, then you have just an indication of what the Lord must feel when we sin. He wants to bless us, but sinning saps the blessings He wants to so freely give. He has given us the choice to follow Him or follow the ways of the world. The latter is far easier to succumb to in a world where sin is constantly all around us. Therefore, we must know Jesus as our Guide, Friend, and even Rescuer. If we truly love Him, then no sin is worth the cost of displeasing Him.

Jesus knows our hearts; He knows everything we are going through. He implores us to look at Him and away from sin, so we can rise above in victory. Sins are just fleeting pleasures, and even if they bring some form of temporary happiness, that is all they are—temporary. Brief pleasures will cause us to lose ground in our walk with Jesus. Jesus offers us the most gratifying pleasure possible—to know Him, the Son of God. No passing sin could ever compare to knowing the Son of God!

We have all sinned and displeased God, so we should not let our pasts keep us from walking forward into a life of freedom and joy in Him. We can ask forgiveness and our sins will be no more, just as we read in Psalm 103:12: **"As far as the east is from the west, so far has He removed our transgressions from us."** With forgiveness, we can begin again on the path He has chosen for us, but we must also recognize that we will have to gain back the ground we have lost. We will have to take the time to make right whatever we did wrong. Thankfully, the Lord's help is only a prayer away and He will show us how to make things right again.

The Lord's love is infinite. **"Greater love has no one than this, that one lay down his life for his friends" (John 15:13).** A true shepherd will lay down his life for his sheep. Jesus, our Shepherd and Guide, did this for us. Because of His love for us, He died so that we might live. He is the truest Friend of all.

Remain faithful to Jesus. The reward of not sinning is that we will be become more like Him with every victory. If we remain faithful to Him, we will find true communion and a new depth of love for Him, making us more determined to stay on the path of life.

The Choice Is Ours

How can we repay the One who paid the ultimate price of dying for our sins? We can touch His heart and live for Him. We have the opportunity to bring Jesus joy by living our lives to please Him. Being pure is a choice. Being righteous is a choice. Living for Him is a choice. It may be hard at times to live such a life, but what greater gift could we give Him?

> WE HAVE ALL SINNED AND DISPLEASED GOD, SO WE SHOULD NOT LET OUR PASTS KEEP US FROM WALKING FORWARD INTO A LIFE OF FREEDOM AND JOY IN HIM.

Jesus has a purpose for all of us. We can never fulfill the totality of what we have been called to do if we are not following the Lord. While spending time with Him, He will reveal details of our purposes and what He wants us to do. The time He has given us is precious, and every breath we breathe is a gift. We must use our time wisely and to the fullest, walking steadily forward upon the path He has chosen for us to follow.

The late Erma Bombeck once said, "When I stand before God at the end of my life, I would hope that I would not have a single bit of talent left and I could say, 'I used everything you gave me.' Then the Lord would say, **'Well done, good and faithful servant'**" (Matthew 25:21 NIV).

We all want to hear those words. We will if we follow the Lord daily on the path of life. When we overcome and are true to Jesus, even when temptations and battles are raging all around us, we will achieve the greatest victory of all in this life: We will bring pleasure to the Lord because we have wholeheartedly followed Him and have accomplished His will for our lives. Additionally, we will receive the highest reward when we at last see Him— we will live forever in constant happiness with Him. There is nothing on this earth that can ever compare to what He is offering us. We simply have to follow Him.

"Let not your heart be troubled; believe in God, believe also in Me.

"In My Father's house are many dwelling places; if it were not so, I would have told you; for I go to prepare a place for you.

"And if I go and prepare a place for you, I will come again, and receive you to Myself; that where I am, there you may be also"(John 14:1-3). ∎

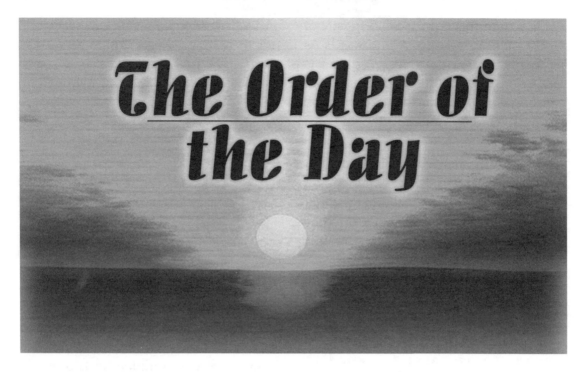

The Order of the Day

All Scriptures are King James Version.

by Steve Thompson

In spite of our modern emphasis on comfort, convenience, and ease, people today are frazzled. Not only unbelievers, but many dedicated believers are just plain weary. This state of weariness is not confined to the elderly or the overworked. It seems almost everyone today talks of being worn-out. Tiredness seems to be the order of the day.

Recently, the Lord showed me that tiredness was the order of the day for many because our day was ordered wrongly. My first thought went to misplaced priorities, and that is partially true. However, the Lord showed me something more foundational about how we live our lives. We have literally reversed the order of the day that God created, and we are experiencing the exact opposite of God's intention for our lives.

God's Order

God never ordained that we would be perpetually wearied and worn-out. His intention is the exact opposite. God wants us to thrive in life, not just survive it. He wants us to be increasingly invigorated through our lives and even through our labor. God has provided for us to have life and to have it abundantly (see John 10:10), not just the things of life, but life itself.

Let's be honest though. Most people, young and old, begin and end their day tired. They wake each morning to enter the workday not refreshed, but looking forward to being done so they can catch some rest. By the time their workday is done, they "crash" or "vegetate," but they do not really find rest. The cycle continues the next day from being less rested than the day before.

In reality, this is the exact opposite of God's plan for our lives. God wants us to thrive, not just survive. So great is His intention that He ordained from the beginning that the structure of the day itself would promote well-being, not tiredness.

In the fifth verse of the Bible there is a small, almost hidden key to experiencing God's intention for our well-being. While keys are small and look insignificant, they make the way for us to enter new realms and realities. Genesis 1:5 provides us with a key to reordering our day and entering the reality of rest and refreshing that God has for us.

> **And God called the light Day, and the darkness he called Night. And the evening and the morning were the first day.**

This verse says that **"the evening and the morning were the first day."** The day that God created starts with the evening and finishes with the morning and daytime. This Scripture provides the foundation for the Jewish day which begins at sundown.

While this may appear to be a seemingly insignificant mention in Scripture, it is really an earth-shattering revelation, which will bring a revolutionary change in our lives. If we adopt God's order of the day, which is opposite of our thinking, consider how profoundly our experience would change.

Reorder Your Day

Our day would begin in the evening, by fellowshipping with those we love. The first thing on God's heart for us is to have communion with our family and to share a meal together. Then after a time of food and fellowship, we rise up, not to work, but to rest and sleep. Then after a full night of rest, we arise not to work, but to another time of fellowship and food with those we love.

> **LET YOUR SOUL FIND DEEP REST IN GOD AND HIS CARE OVER YOUR LIFE.**

Then, after eating twice and fellowshipping with those we love, at the end of our day, we work. We work from being fully rested and refreshed, and are able to give ourselves completely to our work. Now instead of our labor being tainted with the weariness of our souls, it will be impregnated with the joy of life and the presence of God that He intends.

We are encouraged by Paul in Galatians 6:9 to **"not be weary in well doing."** We are called to give ourselves, even more than we are currently, to doing well. But if we will focus first on *being* in Christ, not *doing* for Him, we will end up doing significantly more than if our focus was first set on doing.

Reorder your day, both naturally and spiritually. God's order for you is this: Fellowship with Him and those you love. Have a nice meal—**"taste and see that the Lord is good" (Psalm 34:8).** Rest in God and His mercy toward you—let your soul find deep rest in God and His care over your life. Rise up and have another meal, spiritual and natural, and fellowship again with those you love. Then it's time to work. ■

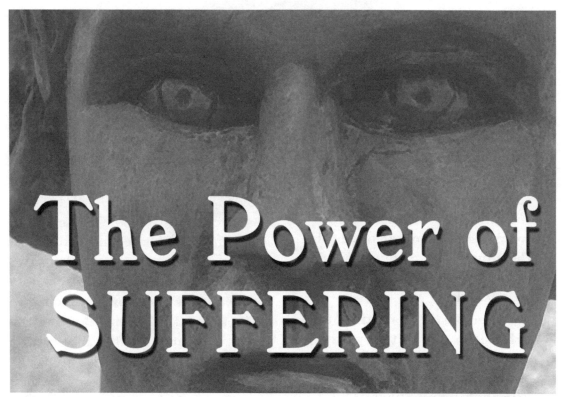

The Power of SUFFERING

All Scriptures are Amplified Version.

by Trevor Tiessen

In western society suffering is not something that is promoted or desired. On the contrary, we do everything we can to avoid it. Even in the church, suffering is not something we usually embrace willingly. While many of us enjoy religious freedom, Jesus reminds us that if they persecuted Him, they will persecute us also (see John 15:20). It is important for us as believers to see the value and power of suffering for the gospel from a biblical standpoint.

Paul and Silas

When we suffer for the sake of the kingdom, the power of the Holy Spirit is released into the earth. Just as worship, prayer, and fasting release the Lord's power, so does suffering for righteousness sake.

In Acts 16 Paul and Silas came to Philippi, a Roman colony in the region of Macedonia. While ministering in this city, they were approached by a slave girl who had a spirit of divination. For several days she had followed Paul and Silas around, shouting out that these men were servants of the Most High God. Finally, Paul commanded the spirit to come out of her.

When the slave girl's owners realized that they had lost their means of income from this girl, they had Paul and Silas stripped, beaten, and thrown in jail. Paul and Silas had done a righteous thing by casting the demon out of this slave girl and they suffered unjustly for it. They were Roman citizens, yet they did not receive a fair trial. Sitting in a jail cell late at night, bloody and beaten with their feet in stocks, they began to do the unthinkable—they began to praise God!

> But about midnight, as Paul and Silas were praying and singing hymns of praise to God, and the [other] prisoners were listening to them,
>
> Suddenly there was a great earthquake, so that the very foundations of the prison were shaken; and at once all the doors were opened and everyone's shackles were unfastened.
>
> When the jailer, startled out of his sleep, saw that the prison doors were open, he drew his sword and was on the point of killing himself, because he supposed that the prisoners had escaped.
>
> But Paul shouted, Do not harm yourself, for we are all here!
>
> Then [the jailer] called for lights and rushed in, and trembling and terrified he fell down before Paul and Silas.
>
> And he brought them out of [the dungeon] and said, Men, what is it necessary for me to do that I may be saved? (Acts 16:25-30)

Under the circumstances, it would have seemed like an opportune time for Paul and Silas to be upset at their injustice, curse the jailer, and feel sorry for themselves. Instead, they not only suffered for righteousness sake, they responded to their suffering in a righteous manor—they praised God. They suffered for doing right and were truly honored and overjoyed to do so.

God's heart was so moved by their willingness to suffer with honor that there was a great earthquake and the jail cells were opened. The shackles not only fell off Paul and Silas, they fell off all the prisoners in the jail! The jailer, who had put them in stocks, knelt at their feet and asked to be saved. Later, not only the jailer was saved, but his whole household as well. Who would have imagined that all this would happen as a result of two men willing to suffer for the gospel? Had Paul and Silas not seen past their own suffering and demanded justice for themselves, it is unlikely that this miracle would have taken place. It is an amazing reality that the salvation of our enemies may depend on our willingness to suffer at their hands.

> God's heart was so moved by their willingness to suffer with honor that there was a great earthquake and the jail cells were opened.

God is not blind to the injustice suffered by His saints. He will move in amazing ways if we choose to lay our lives down for the gospel. Our suffering will not only bring about our deliverance, but the deliverance of others. There are times when it is appropriate to seek justice, but for us as believers, there is a higher way—

the way of righteous suffering that releases the power of God.

Saul's Conversion

Saul of Tarsus, who would later become the Apostle Paul, was a Pharisee zealous for the Law. He relentlessly persecuted the church with violence, throwing both men and women in jail (see Acts 8:3). On his way to Damascus to persecute the church there, Saul had a supernatural encounter with God:

> **He relentlessly persecuted the church with violence, throwing both men and women in jail.**

> **Now as he traveled on, he came near to Damascus, and suddenly a light from heaven flashed around him,**
>
> **and he fell to the ground. Then he heard a voice saying to him, Saul, Saul, why are you persecuting Me [harassing, troubling, and molesting Me]?**
>
> **And Saul said, Who are You, Lord? And He said, I am Jesus, Whom you are persecuting. It is dangerous and it will turn out badly for you to keep kicking against the goad—[to offer vain and perilous resistance].**

> **Trembling and astonished he asked, Lord, what do You desire me to do? The Lord said to him, But arise and go into the city, and you will be told what you must do (Acts 9:3-6).**

This supernatural encounter with the Lord led to Saul's conversion. We know that he was called to be an apostle and a preacher of the gospel (see II Timothy 1:11), but what released this power into his life? He was certainly not seeking this experience himself. Why Saul and not one of the other Pharisees? There are many Christians who have not had an encounter of this magnitude, much less someone who hated the church. The answer is found in Acts 6 and 7.

Stephen, a deacon in the church, was moving in great power and miracles. This provoked an attack by the Jews, who could not refute the miracles or his teaching. As a result, they brought false accusations against him and had him brought before the Sanhedrin (see Acts 6:8-15).

After a discourse on God's history with Israel, Stephen rebuked the Sanhedrin for their resistance to the Holy Spirit, which caused further attack.

> **Then they dragged him out of the city and began to stone him, and the witnesses placed their garments at the feet of a young man named Saul.**
>
> **And while they were stoning Stephen, he prayed, Lord Jesus, receive and accept and welcome my spirit!**
>
> **And falling on his knees, he cried out loudly, Lord, fix not this sin upon them [lay it not to**

their charge!] And when he had said this, he fell asleep in death.

AND SAUL was not only consenting to Stephen's death he was pleased and entirely approving..." (Acts 7:58-60, 8:1).

Stephen not only suffered and died unjustly, he cried out for the Lord to forgive those who were killing him. Stephen's suffering and forgiveness released power from heaven into Saul's life, who was presiding over Stephen's death.

> **Could it be that some of the greatest enemies of the church today are called to be our greatest prophets and apostles?**

Stephen did not live to see the fruit of his suffering, but his suffering and forgiveness resulted in the salvation of one of the greatest Christian leaders of all time. Who would have predicted this prior to Saul's conversion? Could it be that some of the greatest enemies of the church today are called to be our greatest prophets and apostles? Rather than responding with anger and criticism of those who treat us unfairly, should we not love and forgive them and pray that they too are transformed from enemies to allies? Our greatest victory is not to see the wicked punished, but to rescue them from the camp of the enemy and help them become a trophy of God's grace.

Choosing to Suffer

Most of us hate to see injustice. If we had the power to prevent it from happening, we would. It is no wonder that superhero movies are so popular. It is inspiring to see a hero use his supernatural powers to thwart evil and bring about justice. But what if we had the supernatural power to prevent our suffering and refrained from using it? That seems preposterous, but that is exactly what Jesus did.

> **And behold, one of those who were with Jesus reached out his hand and drew his sword and, striking the body servant of the high priest, cut off his ear.**
>
> **Then Jesus said to him, Put your sword back into its place, for all who draw the sword will die by the sword.**
>
> **Do you suppose that I cannot appeal to My Father, and He will immediately provide Me with more than twelve legions [more than 80,000] of angels?**
>
> **But how then would the Scriptures be fulfilled, that it must come about this way? (Matthew 26:51-54)**

Jesus was not a victim. He had very real power to save His own life. Legions of angels were at His disposal. He had the power at any given moment, right up until His crucifixion, to deliver Himself, but He chose not to. How many of us, with that kind of power, would freely choose to suffer? For the joy set before

Him, He endured the cross, knowing that multitudes would be saved as a result of His obedience to the Father. He could see past His suffering and know that it was worth it. Jesus had an eternal perspective, not a temporal one.

It is interesting to note that He also refused Peter's help, when he drew his sword to defend Jesus. Peter's intent to protect Jesus could certainly be understood. Most of us would have been inclined to act in a similar fashion, yet when Peter drew his sword to fight, the Lord told him to put it down. Jesus did not need Peter's help. Furthermore, Peter's actions were in direct conflict with God's plan. How many of us could have understood this at the time it was happening? God's ways are certainly above our ways. It actually would have been a disaster if Peter had "successfully" defended Jesus.

Not only do we need to be careful about taking up justice for ourselves, we need to be careful about letting other people come to our defense. It is not usually in the best interest of the kingdom for someone to take up our offenses. If we are permitting people to take up our offenses, it shows that we are still trying to hold on to our rights. To endure suffering, we must be prepared to lay down our rights.

In John 19:10-11, Jesus affirms that He is not simply a victim of circumstance.

So Pilate said to Him, Will You not speak [even] to me? Do You not know that I have power (authority) to release You and I have power to crucify You?

Jesus answered, You would not have any power or authority whatsoever against (over) Me if it were not given you from above. For this reason the sin and guilt of the one who delivered Me over to you is greater.

Jesus understood that He was not a victim of the authorities, but that His Father was really in control. Jesus still had the power to deliver Himself, but chose to remain in submission to the Father's will. He did not blame Pilate or the Jews for His situation, but recognized that He was called to suffer at their hands.

> **Not only do we need to be careful about taking up justice for ourselves, we need to be careful about letting other people come to our defense.**

Without the understanding that Jesus had, most us would be doing everything we could to get out of a situation like this. We would be appealing to the Lord to deliver us. There may be times when the Lord delivers us from trouble, but at other times it may actually be the Father's will for us to suffer at the hands of others to bring about a victory for the kingdom. As believers we need to recognize that the Father cares about our welfare and is in control. If we are either protected from or delivered into suffering, it is not at random. Jesus trusted the Father with His life and so can we.

> **The power released through His suffering resulted not only in the supernatural occurrences at His crucifixion, but in salvation and healing for the whole world.**

The Ultimate Injustice

Jesus was completely innocent, yet suffered terribly at the hands of wicked men. He had broken no laws, but He suffered as a criminal. He was arrested, beaten, cursed, spat on, had His beard ripped out, and was forced to wear a crown of thorns. He was then taken outside Jerusalem where He was crucified. Although Jesus had the power to deliver Himself, He not only allowed this to take place, He forgave those who stood by and sneered as He died on the cross.

Power is released when we suffer for righteousness sake. When Jesus died on the cross, there was an immediate release of power.

> **And Jesus cried again with a loud voice and gave up His spirit.**
>
> **And at once the curtain of the sanctuary of the temple was torn in two from top to bottom; the earth shook and the rocks were split.**
>
> **The tombs were opened and many bodies of the saints who had fallen asleep in death were raised [to life];**
>
> **And coming out of the tombs after His resurrection, they went into the holy city and appeared to many people.**
>
> **When the centurion and those who were with him keeping watch over Jesus observed the earthquake and all that was happening, they were terribly frightened and filled with awe, and said, Truly this was God's Son! (Matthew 27:50-54)**

The suffering of Jesus caused an earthquake, raised people from the dead, and the veil of the temple was torn in two. The greater the suffering, the greater the release of power. What looked like a defeat for the kingdom was actually the greatest victory of all time.

The ultimate injustice was the persecution and crucifixion of the Lord Jesus. He was the spotless Lamb of God, without sin or blemish. He was the perfect representation of the Father to a fallen world that hated and rejected Him. The power released through His suffering resulted not only in the supernatural occurrences at His crucifixion, but in salvation and healing for the whole world, for everyone who calls upon His name. The words of Isaiah were most certainly fulfilled by our Messiah:

> **Surely He has borne our griefs (sicknesses, weaknesses, and distresses) and carried our**

sorrows and pains [of punishment], yet we [ignorantly] considered Him stricken, smitten, and afflicted by God [as if with leprosy].

But He was wounded for our transgressions, He was bruised for our guilt and iniquities; the chastisement [needful to obtain] peace and well-being for us was upon Him, and with the stripes [that wounded] Him we are healed and made whole.

All we like sheep have gone astray, we have turned every one to his own way; and the Lord has made to light upon Him the guilt and iniquity of us all (Isaiah 53:4-6).

> Rather than see our enemies punished, let us forgive and see them touched by the power of God.

Summary

As we endure suffering as Christians, whether it is false accusations, injustice, or any other kind of offense, let us not forget the greater good that is at stake. Jesus laid His life down for those who hated Him, and so must we. Rather than see our enemies punished, let us forgive and see them touched by the power of God.

The enemy cannot win. If we receive justice, we can be thankful. If we suffer injustice, power from heaven will be released and his plan will backfire. Let us take joy in persecution and consider ourselves honored to suffer for the sake of the gospel. Whether we live to see the fruit of our suffering or not, let us not forget the eternal perspective that the Lord has given us.

Blessed and happy and enviably fortunate and spiritually prosperous (in the state in which the born-again child of God enjoys and finds satisfaction in God's favor and salvation, regardless of his outward conditions) are those who are persecuted for righteousness' sake (for being and doing right), for theirs is the kingdom of heaven!

Blessed (happy, to be envied, and spiritually prosperous—with life-joy and satisfaction in God's favor and salvation, regardless of your outward conditions) are you when people revile you and persecute you and say all kinds of evil things against you falsely on My account.

Be glad and supremely joyful, for your reward in heaven is great (strong and intense), for in this same way people persecuted the prophets who before you (Matthew 5:10-12). ■

Being Conformed to His Image

All Scriptures are New King James Version.

by Robin McMillan

Paul the apostle had an amazing revelation of the eternal purpose of God.

> **For whom He foreknew, He also predestined to be conformed to the image of His Son, that He might be the firstborn among many brethren (Romans 8:29).**

God wants many other children who are like His Son Jesus in their very nature. It is not an outward conformity that God desires where two people look, act, or dress alike, but an inner one where our lives are empowered by the very life of the Son of God who dwells inside us. This is what it means for Christ *to be* our lives.

> **When Christ *who is our life* appears, then you also will appear with Him in glory (Colossians 3:4).**

Living this way is not automatic. While the salvation experience is instant and justification comes by faith, being conformed to the image of Christ is a process. It is achieved over time as we yield to God in the specific dealings He has designed for each of us.

One popular method of living like Christ involves asking in any given situation, "What would Jesus do?" and then behaving accordingly. This method gives us a practical guide on how to respond in certain situations. However, being conformed to the image of Jesus is something that must occur on a much deeper level. Our lives must embody Christ's life flowing through us. We should fit together like a hand fits inside a glove. This process of breaking and being molded to the "hand of God" is similar to the way a baseball glove is prepared to conform to the player's hand.

Noah Liberman's book, *Glove Affairs, The Romance, History, and Tradition of the Baseball Glove,* describes the process of how a baseball glove endures to conform to the hand of the player who owns it in order to fulfill the purpose for its creation. Particularly in the early days of baseball's history, gloves were stiff and stubborn and required an extensive process to change them into useable and reliable pieces of equipment. This process provides a prophetic picture of the things we go through to be conformed to the image of Christ.

The Process of Conforming

Will Wedge, a reporter for the *New York Sun,* wrote the following article in 1925 that described one process used by the New York Yankees professional baseball team to break in a glove:

> The Yankees are fortunate in having one of the best glove doctors in the majors. He is [former major leaguer] Charley O'Leary...He can take a glove that is inclined to buck and shy at grounders and break it in like a Western cowboy and rodeo rider would break in a bad tempered bronco...It's said he whispers things into the fingers of stiff and unwieldy gloves that gives them the secret of snaring everything that comes their way...He takes gloves apart and rebuilds them nearer the heart's and fingers' desire. He unlaces the new glove and amputates excess padding...It is really the way Charley talks to a glove and discusses things with it that makes it the dapper and well-groomed object it becomes when he has finished with it...(Glove Affairs, page 35-37).

Yogi Berra

Yogi Berra, the enigmatic Hall of Fame catcher for the New York Yankees played from 1946 to 1965. He had his own patented method of breaking in a catcher's mitt before it was suitable for use:

> Just put [the mitt] in the whirlpool, soak it, until it stops bubbling. Wrap balls in it with rubber bands. Then dry it out. We used to have a clothes dryer. It was like a heater. Put [the mitt] in there for two or three days (page 39).

Bill Davis

Bill Davis of Lorton, Virginia, a current glove collector, was once a bat-boy for the Philadelphia Phillies in the 1960s. Part of his duty was to assist the players, one of whom asked him to break in his new glove. Davis did not know exactly how to do it and "was working on it in the dugout when Jim Busby, then coach of the Astros, came up. He said, "Kid, let me show you how to break in a mitt." He then proceeded to pound the daylights out of the glove with a baseball bat" (page 40).

Ron Santo

Ron Santo, a five time Gold Glove award winning third baseman had his own method:

> I would put two baseballs in it, wrap it real tight with string and then put it in water and let it sit all night, take it out the next day and let it dry out. Then I would go play catch with it. And I would keep spitting in it, and after the

first day get it kind of soft in the pocket but leave it firm on the outside. Then I'd put oil on it in the pocket (page 40).

Ouch!

These unorthodox methods were typical ways both professional and amateur ballplayers prepared their gloves for playing the game. Unfortunately, people are a lot like new baseball gloves—stiff, stubborn, and un-pliable. We must often experience extreme circumstances before we effectively yield to the life God has already put within us.

Spiritual Parallels

This "breaking in" process of a baseball glove has amazing similarities to our spiritual development. Hebrews 12:5-6 contains a promise most of us are not anxious to claim:

> **"My son, do not despise the chastening of the LORD, nor be discouraged when you are rebuked by Him;**
>
> **for whom the LORD loves He chastens, and scourges every son whom He receives."**

Scourging is a painful process, one God promised that every son would experience. His chastening is not a sign of rejection but one of the surest signs of His love for us. His purpose is that we profit from His attention and are fully trained in the way of righteousness. The writer of Hebrews alerts us to this truth about God so that we will not **"become weary and discouraged in our souls"** (see **Hebrews 12:3**) and reminds us that even Jesus Himself endured great hardships and adversity yet was without sin.

Confinement

Most ballplayers break in their gloves using confinement and restriction. They tie the glove around several baseballs to forge a re-shaping that make it better suited to catch the ball. God often uses confining circumstances to help us conform to His purpose. Sometimes the confinement is disciplinary, because we do not want what the Lord wants for us, or we are not listening to Him. He uses the confinement to get our attention and speak to us. However in many cases there is no rebellion or sin involved; but, like a young sapling or tomato plant, we are tied and grounded to ensure our proper growth and development.

Charlie O'Leary's method involved speaking to the gloves as he took them apart and put them back together. This, too, describes how many people feel in the discipline of the Lord, as they are taken apart and put back together. Even then, the Lord is quick to speak and encourage us.

The prophet Hosea describes this process in chapter 2:14-15 of his book:

> **"Therefore, behold, I will allure her, will bring her into the wilderness, and speak comfort to her.**
>
> **I will give her her vineyards from there, and the Valley of**

Achor as a door of hope; she shall sing there...

God reveals His ultimate purpose of securing the hearts and love of His people, even if it means bringing them into a place of distress. In that needy place they discover God's abundant provision, even fruitful places like vineyards and places of renewed hope. The Valley of Achor means the valley of tribulation. When we discover that God can provide hope in times of the worst trouble, we are encouraged to know that He can do anything. Even there His people will learn to trust and depend upon Him alone. This, too, is part of the process of being conformed to the image of His Son.

Circumcision

O'Leary would also amputate part of the padding if it made the glove awkward or hindered its effectiveness. This speaks of the circumcision of the flesh, the cutting away of those attitudes and actions that every believer must experience.

In Him you were also circumcised with the circumcision made without hands, by putting off the body of the sins of the flesh, by the circumcision of Christ (Colossians 2:11).

That ongoing experience is part of our identification with Christ and His death, burial, and resurrection. Without the cutting away, the new growth will not bear its maximum fruit.

Soaking

Many ballplayers soaked their gloves in water to make them change their shape. Soaking causes the fibers in the leather to separate, adapt to the change in form, then relink when they dry. This soaking process speaks of two things—applying the life-altering Word of God to our lives, and spending time in the presence of the Lord. Both are absolutely necessary.

The Water of the Word

We truly need to soak in the Word of God. We know from Ephesians 5:25-27 that the washing of the water of the Word is vital:

Husbands, love your wives, just as Christ also loved the church and gave Himself for her,

that He might sanctify and cleanse her with the washing of water by the word,

that He might present her to Himself a glorious church, not having spot or wrinkle or any such thing, but that she should be holy and without blemish.

The washing of the water of the Word sanctifies and cleanses the church of its spots and wrinkles, becoming functionally holy and flawless. That is the kind of bride the Father wants His Son to have.

Psalm 37: Soaking in His Presence

Psalm 37 describes the practical way to soak in the presence of the Lord.

Do not fret because of evil-doers, nor be envious of the workers of iniquity.

For they shall soon be cut down like the grass, and wither as the green herb.

Trust in the LORD, and do good; dwell in the land, and feed on His faithfulness.

Delight yourself also in the LORD, and He shall give you the desires of your heart.

Commit your way to the LORD, trust also in Him, and He shall bring it to pass.

He shall bring forth your righteousness as the light, and your justice as the noonday.

Rest in the LORD, and wait patiently for Him; do not fret because of him who prospers in his way, because of the man who brings wicked schemes to pass.

Cease from anger, and forsake wrath; do not fret—it only causes harm" (Psalm 37:1-8).

First of all we must not fret, a word meaning "to worry continually about something." Instead, we should trust in the Lord, do good, and feed on the facts of His faithfulness. To be even more saturated by Him, we should delight ourselves in Him, commit our ways to Him, and rest in Him. The natural result of this process is that the Lord gives us the very desires of our hearts and brings out of us and through us both righteousness and justice, as bright as the noonday sun. We must soak in the Lord to be conformed to the image of His Son.

Constant Use

For a glove to be reliable in a game, it needs to be used consistently beforehand. We are the same way. Until we function consistently in our purpose, we never become fully proficient in it.

> TO BE EVEN MORE SATURATED BY HIM, WE SHOULD DELIGHT OURSELVES IN HIM, COMMIT OUR WAYS TO HIM, AND REST IN HIM.

Jesus understood from a young age that He had a job to do and sought to accomplish it. At the age of twelve He went with His family to Jerusalem to celebrate the Feast of Passover. When the family party returned home, Jesus remained in the city. After three days His parents found Him in the temple asking questions and listening to the priests. When His parents questioned Him about His behavior, Jesus said:

"Why did you seek Me? Did you not know that I must be about My Father's business?" (Luke 2:49)

At the age of twelve Jesus was already engaged in His purpose. By the age of thirty-three He would conclude:

"I have glorified You on the earth. I have finished the work which You have given Me to do" (John 17:4).

We, too, should have the same perspective and live to finish the work the Father has given us to do.

Oiled

A significant part of the preparation of any baseball glove is the periodic application of oil. The oil softens the pores of the leather enabling the glove to maintain its shape and durability. We, too, must be "oiled," anointed with the Spirit of God to live as He has called us to live. Without that oil we become hard, then brittle, begin to lose our shape and, eventually the inward presence and power of the Lord.

Each Player's Loyalty to His Glove

Professional ballplayers have a peculiar possessiveness and loyalty about their gloves. They almost become an extension of their body and personality. One famous third basemen, Brooks Robinson of the Baltimore Orioles, refused to replace his worn-out model. Ira Beckow of the *New York Times* found it to be hideous. *"He described a cracked pocket, ripped insides, dark and shrunken wool padding, a small, dirty piece of tape along the heel and another on the web, the whole thing 'a tobacco-juice brown'"* (page 44).

Phil Rizzuto, an infielder with the Yankees, kept the same glove for fourteen years, but he sent it to the Rawlings factory each off season for repairs. *"He probably played 14 years with the same glove. At least he looked on it as being the same glove,"* says Roger Lueckenhoff, a Rawlings glove executive for forty-two years, until 1933. *"[Glove designer] Harry Latine would refurbish it every year and replace parts, and he kept gradually replacing parts to where it was a new glove, but in Rizutto's mind it was the same glove"* (pages 46-47).

> **WITHOUT THAT OIL WE BECOME HARD, THEN BRITTLE, BEGIN TO LOSE OUR SHAPE AND, EVENTUALLY THE INWARD PRESENCE AND POWER OF THE LORD.**

I grew up playing sports in a highly competitive family where both parents coached and played sports on the college level. I began playing ball when I was nine years old and did not stop until after my freshman year in college. I, too, had a special glove. As a ten-year old sportsman, my parents gave me a Wilson catcher's mitt for Christmas. It was a Del Crandall turtle-back model. It was called a turtle-back because when turned upside down it looked like a turtle.

The glove instantly became my prized possession. I was mesmerized by the feel of it on my hand, the smell of the leather, and the sound of the baseball as it "thwacked" loudly into the pocket when I caught it. When I wore the glove, in my mind I was instantly in the World Series catching Whitey Ford's pitches for the New York Yankees as we beat the Cardinals or the Dodgers, or whoever else dared to challenge our supremacy.

> **GOD NUMBERS OUR WANDERINGS, PUTS OUR TEARS IN A SPECIAL BOTTLE, AND RECORDS ALL OUR ACTIVITIES IN ONE OF HIS BOOKS!**

I played with it day and night. It was rarely out of my sight. Even when at bat I was aware of where it sat by the bench near my other equipment. When it got dirty, I cleaned it with saddle soap and oiled it with either olive oil (smelled too bad!), or neat's foot oil to be sure it stayed in top shape. At night it did not stay in the closet or on a shelf somewhere. For the first year or so it stayed safely in bed with me right next to my pillow.

The love of a child for his first baseball glove, and the love of God for a specific person may be a weak analogy, but both are very personal and heartfelt. In each case, because of great affection and delight, the smallest peculiarities and nuances do not go unnoticed.

As I looked at my glove I could remember each scar on it and what event caused it. "Oh, that slash happened when Ben tried to steal home and I cut him down at the plate. Man was that a collision!" God knows much more about us and records all of it. Jesus said: **"the very hairs of your head are all numbered" (Matthew 10:30).** Furthermore, God numbers our wanderings, puts our tears in a special bottle, and records all our activities in one of His books! (see Psalm 56:8). What kind of God is He Who keeps up with such insignificant aspects of our being? The kind we have!

In Conclusion

Being conformed to the image of His Son is much more than getting saved; it is a lifelong pursuit. In Galatians 4:19, Paul expressed the deep desire of his heart for those he had introduced to the Lord:

> **My little children, for whom I labor in birth again until Christ is formed in you.**

He wanted them to be like Jesus. He also wanted the same thing for himself and pursued it with all his heart. He never claimed to have arrived, but he knew he was on his way and that he lived a life in hot pursuit of this goal. His own words confirm it:

> **Not that I have already attained, or am already perfected; but I press on, that I may lay hold of that for which Christ Jesus has also laid hold of me.**

> **Brethren, I do not count myself to have apprehended; but one thing I do, forgetting those things which are behind and reaching forward to those things which are ahead,**

> **I press toward the goal for the prize of the upward call of God in Christ Jesus (Philippians 3:12-14).**

Though we may be predestined to bear the image of His Son, if we do not yield ourselves to the process, it will never fully happen. If we understand the necessity of this process, we will more readily embrace the dealings of the Lord and progress in the Christian life. We must press on. ■

Quotations taken from *Glove Affairs, The Romance, History, and Tradition of the Baseball Glove*, Noah Liberman, Triumph Books, Chicago, IL, 2003.

To some, this word discipline will have a monastic flavor, for it smells of the Middle Ages or throws onto the screen of the mind a picture of an unwashed hermit or a hollow-eyed anchorite. Be not deceived. Every smart "top brass" military expert has arrived there because he wore the harness of discipline.

—Leonard Ravenhill

Mustard Seeds of Wisdom

TURNING A VISITATION INTO A HABITATION

All Scriptures are New King James Version.

by Paul Goulet

Have you ever experienced a great move of God in your church, youth group, or during a retreat? If you are like the thousands of people that I have seen through the years, the pressing question that troubles all of us is: "Why did the move of God stop?" "Why was it so brief?"

So many wonder what they could have done to continue this visitation of the Holy Spirit. Others speak wistfully about these visitations, wrongfully concluding that their short-term nature is unavoidable. The purpose of this article is to discuss the incredible details of a sustained move of God in Las Vegas, Nevada. It is not my purpose to present our experiences as the norm. I encourage you to read our experience prayerfully. Ask the Holy Spirit to give you divine applications to your life and your ministry.

In 1992, my wife Denise and I assumed the leadership of a small church in Las Vegas, Nevada. All of my training was in psychology and pastoral counseling. Consequently, I felt woefully inadequate for the tasks of being a senior pastor. As a result of my feelings of insecurity, I started fasting one day a week, while I prayed on a mountain or in the desert.

In October of 1994, during one of these days on the mountain, the Lord touched me in ways my graduate degree could not explain. Urged by a member of our congregation, we attended a pastor's conference in Canada that opened our eyes to the explosive power of God. I like to identify this type of power as a *dynamite encounter.* In Acts 1:8, this power, *dunamis[1]* is promised to the believers. God introduced me to this type of power on the last night of this Canadian Leaders' Conference.

I will never forget how my life was dramatically altered when I asked God to bring revival to my city. Only God could bring revival to Las Vegas. Some might call it a modern-day Sodom. I would prefer to think of it as a Nineveh that is going to repent and change. That fateful night found me at the altar asking a leader to pray for my city. Instead of praying for Las Vegas, he insisted on praying for me. At first I refused, but then I opened myself to a powerful visitation from the Holy Spirit.

On my first Sunday back in Las Vegas, the power of God touched our church. This move of God lasted a few weeks. Not everyone in our church received the Holy Spirit with open arms. As the pastor, I also felt confused by the controversy and I was afraid of the fallout. Eventually, I asked the Holy Spirit to stop touching me with this great power because I felt so out of control. To my surprise, everything supernatural seemed to stop completely.

The Holy Spirit came because I asked for revival. But when He came He was not welcomed. After a few months of silence, I realized I had made a dreadful mistake. Motivated by my personal pride and a desire to please people, I had grieved the Holy Spirit. Instead of fighting me, the Holy Spirit backed off. I assume that He has done this in many churches. Perhaps the Holy Spirit has discovered that pastors

---

[1]Spirit Filled Bible, New King James Version © 2002
dunamis: **energy, power, might, great force, great ability, strength**

and leaders want Him to visit, but they are unwilling for Him to move in. The pain and the shame of my error caused me to review my mistakes, repent of my sins, and pray for a second chance.

ONLY GOD COULD BRING REVIVAL TO LAS VEGAS.

During the absence of visible power and miracles, the church started to grow again. We acquired fifteen acres on the highway and built our first series of buildings. It amazed me that God was so gracious. In spite of my rejection of His Spirit, He still blessed and added to the church. Eighteen months later, He also gave me a second chance. During a conference for pastors, Claudio Freidzon gave a word of knowledge that someone had been praying for a second chance. As I ran to the altar, my expectations were met by a merciful Holy Spirit who touched me with His dynamite again. I did not just want a touch, I wanted to be transformed and used. I will never forget the question God asked me as I lay on the ground: "Paul, do you really want My power?" "Yes Lord," was my answer. He then said, "Ok, but this time you must die."

The vision that transfixed me for the next few minutes is forever branded on my mind. I saw my left hand being pierced by a nail. I was being nailed to a sinner's cross. As the blood poured from my hand, God started to list my sins and ask me if I was willing to die to them. One by one I saw them written on a scroll that hung below my hand. I wept for almost two hours. I agreed to die to people-pleasing, pride, anger, lust, selfish ambitions, and other issues. Paul understands what I went through that night:

I have been crucified with Christ; it is no longer I who live, but Christ lives in me; and the life which I now live in the flesh I live by faith in the Son of God, who loved me and gave Himself for me (Galatians 2:20.)

Likewise you also, reckon yourselves to be dead indeed to sin, but alive to God in Christ Jesus our Lord (Romans 6:11).

Claudio frequently returned to my prostrate position with exhortations of "Reciblo" and "Mas, Senor, mas!" The power that touched me that night was unbelievable. I had committed to do whatever it took to keep this power and learn whatever I needed to learn.

The past eight years have been a journey that Paul described in Philippians 3:10: **"...that I may know Him and the power of His resurrection, and the fellowship of His sufferings, being conformed to His death..."**

The word **"know"** is a very specific Greek term that means an intimate knowledge. It is *ginosko*, which is how God deserves to be known. A life of discovery will never exhaust this desire.

I have been married for twenty-four years. Denise and I both testify that the journey of discovery continues even to this day. What a great journey! Through its ups and downs and successes and failures in this relationship, we have invested into weekly dates, counseling, marriage retreats, and heart-to-heart talks. Our intimate relationship with the Holy Spirit, with His power, and with His sufferings will never cease. I realized that not only did I need to repent for grieving Him, but I also had to confess my failures to the church.

> **OUR JOURNEY OF REDISCOVERY WITH THE HOLY SPIRIT HAS ENABLED US TO CONTINUE TO GROW BOTH IN NUMBERS AND MATURITY.**

On my first Sunday back from the conference, I asked for forgiveness and pledged to surrender every service to the Holy Spirit. I invited all of those that were interested to return that evening for a time of impartation.

Roman 1:11 provided me with a biblical framework to help me understand what I had experienced. Our journey of rediscovery with the Holy Spirit has enabled us to continue to grow both in numbers and maturity. The purpose of this article is to underline seven principles to which we attribute our ongoing revival at International Church of Las Vegas. We have discovered seven priorities that have kept us on course to a lifelong journey of the Holy Spirit. It is my prayer that these seven priorities will become a source of inspiration and guidance for turning a visitation into a habitation of the Holy Spirit.

It is our deepest desire to have the Holy Spirit turn your church or ministry in a habitation of the Lord. We do not want misplaced priorities to be an end to this move of God. I am sure that you feel the same way.

#1 Priority: Keep Soul Winning as Your Priority.

As the Holy Spirit filled our services with His power, we reminded the people of the purpose for this outpouring. Acts 1:8 is so very clear about this issue: **"But you shall receive power when the Holy Spirit has come upon you; and you shall be witnesses to Me in Jerusalem, and in all Judea and Samaria, and to the end of the earth."**

The ultimate purpose of the Holy Spirit is to fill us in power so that we can reach the lost for Christ. It is very easy to get caught up with the initial response to a visitation of God. The falling, crying, and other reactions to His presence are only temporary. We cannot pitch our tents around physical reactions to the supernatural presence. In I Corinthians 12:7, Paul explains that there is a difference between a reaction to the Holy Spirit and a manifestation of the Holy Spirit: **"But the manifestation of the Spirit is given to each one for the profit of all."**

The Greek word used for **"manifestation"** is *emphanidzo*, which means "to cause to shine, to appear, to reveal, to come to view, to exhibit or make known."

The manifestation of the Holy Spirit is the way He shines through people for the good of the body of Christ and the world. The initial physical reaction depends more upon each person's personality and needs.

When the wind of the Holy Spirit blows, we all respond differently. Some of us are oak trees, others are weeping willows, but all of us are called to reach the world. At ICLV we do not emphasize falling down or standing up; we emphasize the purpose of the infusion of the Spirit of God. We are not concerned about whether people feel the Holy Spirit, but whether they receive what He is depositing at the altar.

I have seen many Christians get stuck at one response to the power of God, instead of allowing His power to equip them to bear much fruit.

#2 Priority: Keep Intimacy With Christ and His Power as Your Focus.

As we have become intimate with His power, we have discovered that God fills us with different types of power for different purposes. Many of us are familiar with the four Greek words that are translated as love in our English version: agape, eros, phileo, and storgi. Each word has a distinctive meaning that is lost in English. In like manner, the word "power" is used for five different Greek words that are unique.

Let us take some time to study these words because they play a huge role in revivals worldwide.

A. Dunamis

In Acts 1:8, we were introduced to the Greek word *dunamis*, meaning "energy, power, might, great force, great ability, strength." This type of power filled the disciples on the Day of Pentecost.

That day was marked by an earthquake, tongues of fire, and a mighty wind. There was such a commotion that it drew a large crowd. Was it the one hundred twenty who were speaking in tongues and prophesying, or was it the way they walked that caused the people to think that they were drunk?

It seems clear that when God fills people with the *dunamis,* signs and wonders usually follow. In our services, we have seen the *dunamis* touch and deliver thousands.

In many Pentecostal circles, this expectation that *dunamis* will touch people is very common. In fact, if this does not occur, they believe that God has not moved.

B. Exousia

Mark 3:14-15: **"Then He appointed twelve, that they might be with Him and that He might send them out to preach, and to have power to heal sicknesses and to cast out demons."** A move of God is always marked by the power of God being deposited in the lives of His servants. In Mark 3:14-15, Jesus imparted a type of power that would enable them to use His *dunamis. Exousia* is the authority or right to act. It is the ability or capacity to do something. In this passage, Jesus imparted authority, described their mission, and received reports of their success.

For a revival to continue for years or generations, every believer needs to receive a divine impartation of authority.

We are talking about the priesthood of believers being empowered to change the world. We are talking about the key ingredient to Ephesians 4:11-12. If every believer in your church walks in diverse authority, God will heal the sick, save the lost, and deliver the oppressed.

C. Energes

Hebrews 4:12 says **"For the word of God is living and powerful, and sharper than any two-edged sword, piercing even to the division of soul and spirit, and of joints and marrow, and is a discerner of the thoughts and intents of the heart."** Have you ever been engaged by the Word of God or by a Spirit-led sermon? In Hebrews 4:12, the author uses the word *energes* to describe a unique type of power. It means that "something is at work." We get our word energetic from it. It is active and effective.

It is important to understand that when we ask God for power He may answer us with what we need most. If we need dynamite, He will explode into our lives. If we need authority, He will give us *exousia*. If we need more energy and inspiration, He will give us *energes*.

A church in revival will need different types of power at different times. The Spirit-filled walk should never be boring! Every day should be a day of discovery.

D. Kratos

which He will manifest in His own time, He who is the blessed and only Potentate, the King of kings and Lord of lords,

who alone has immortality, dwelling in unapproachable

light, whom no man has seen or can see, to whom be honor and everlasting power. Amen (I Timothy 6:15-16).

Kratos refers to the dominion strength and manifested power that the Lord exerts in this world. Could it be that He would also fill us with this dominion power? Isn't this the level of power that the disciples worked with as they turned the world upside down? Haven't we been called to rule and reign with Him?

A few years ago I chose over a dozen businessmen to mentor and train. I believe that everybody needs a prophet or priest or pastor to help them spiritually, emotionally, relationally, and practically. The prophet, Nathan, played this role in David's life in II Samuel 12. My primary objective was to help these businessmen take dominion, to rule and reign as kings and priests. In just a few years, I have seen this happen.

I am convinced that God wants to pour His *kratos* power into believers and the church as a whole. How else could we change cities and transform nations? How else can a man lead his family and business? How else can a mother receive the ability to lead her home?

E. Ischuros

II Corinthians 10:10: **"For his letters,"** they say, **"are weighty and powerful, but his bodily presence is weak, and his speech contemptible."** *Ischuros* means great strength. When was the last time that you needed a dose of great strength? Paul's letters to the Corinthian church were full of great strength. In our generation, we need great strength to confront

problems in our families, cities, and around the world. We need great strength to face our challenges. We need great strength to confront corruption even in the church. We need great strength to start ministries, to confront wolves, and to keep the flames of revival burning.

#3 Priority: Keep the Vision Clear.

II Corinthians 3:18 says: **"But we all, with unveiled face, beholding as in a mirror the glory of the Lord, are being transformed into the same image from glory to glory, just as by the Spirit of the Lord."** Real revivals continue for generations when the vision is clear. The vision has to be other-people centered. The vision must include strong venues of discipleship such as home cells or small group Bible studies.

The vision must contain opportunities for service to God. Everyone can find their place of service in the body of Christ. What is the vision for your life, family, and church? Is it a God-breathed vision?

#4 Priority: Keep the Altars Safe.

The safety of your altars will be an important element in the ongoing outpouring of the Spirit. Having well-trained altar workers who are led by the Spirit is important. Here are a few guidelines that have helped keep our altars safe.

1. Men pray with men; women pray with women.
2. No pushing or shoving to cause people to fall.
3. Only trained leaders can minister at the altar.

#5 Priority: Keep the Word and Worship as Center.

Although we have had incredible times at the altar with people being healed, saved, and delivered, we always prioritize the need to worship God and the need to hear the Word of God.

Many churches have done away with true worship. We firmly believe that worship is the open door to His presence and His power. No matter what may happen in a service, we always include a time of preaching or teaching from the Word. People want to experience the power of God but they also need to experience the power of the Word.

#6 Keep the Leadership Pure.

Scripture warns us that there are three real dangers to our continued revival: **"the lust of the flesh, the lust of the eyes, and the pride of life,"** found in I John 2:16. The anointing and power of the Holy Spirit can be very exciting. He can open wonderful doors of blessing and influence. However, leaders can take advantage of this power. They can try to use it to manipulate people or take advantage of them. Strong accountability is required to keep our teams pure. We do not want to defile the holiness of a great move of God.

#7 Stay Flexible to the Holy Spirit.

Jesus taught His disciples to remain open and flexible to the Holy Spirit. In John 14:16, Jesus prophesied that the Holy Spirit would come in the form of a Comforter: **"And I will pray the Father, and he shall give you another Comforter, that he may abide with you for ever"** (KJV). In John 14:17, He would come as the Spirit of truth: **"Even the Spirit of truth; whom the world cannot receive, because it seeth him not, neither knoweth him: but ye know him; for he dwelleth with you, and shall be in you"** (KJV). In John 14:26 He reveals Himself as a teacher: **"But the Helper, the Holy Spirit, whom the Father will send in My name, He will teach you all things, and bring to your remembrance all things that I said to you."** In John 16:7, He proves to be a true helper: **"Nevertheless I tell you the truth. It is to your advantage that I go away; for if I do not go away, the Helper will not come to you; but if I depart, I will send Him to you."** As we remain submitted to the Holy Spirit, He will minister to every person in our services in a unique way: His way.

Conclusion

A Spirit-filled life is a life of revival. A Spirit-filled church is one of continued growth and maturity. An outpouring of the Holy Spirit does not have to be short-lived. It can surely lead us from glory to glory: **"But we all, with unveiled face, beholding as in a mirror the glory of the Lord, are being transformed into the same image from glory to glory, just as by the Spirit of the Lord"** (II Corinthians 3:18).

Ephesians 3:20-21 explains so clearly what our lives should look like: **"Now to Him who is able to do exceedingly abundantly above all that we ask or think, according to the power that works in us, to Him be glory in the church by Christ Jesus to all generations, forever and ever. Amen."** I challenge you to embrace nothing less and to expect so much more. ■

Marked by the LORD

All Scriptures are New King James Version unless otherwise indicated.

by John Paul Jackson

God's name is our heritage, our authority, and our hope. It is our very life essence—a part of God's glory we need desperately. His name, and the fullness that comes with it, must be seared into our very being. To carry it properly, we must have character above reproach, standing pure and holy before Him.

God is calling us to be a people marked by His name, to become willing vessels who have removed any unconsecrated things from our lives and unholy affections from our hearts.

We will be stretched and will have to deal with new issues that He reveals to us as we grow daily in Him. While our friends may get away with certain behaviors, God will call us to a higher standard of holiness and morality. His name needs to become dearer to us than anything else.

The Mark of Consecration

In order for God to create the necessary consecration in our lives, He will have to help us in submitting different levels of our lives to Him. God wants to align our hearts more perfectly with His. He desires for us to shed any affection that might steal away our hearts' focus from Him. Our lives need to be consecrated at this level of thinking: A consecrated life has learned to focus its thoughts on whatever is pure, right, holy, and good (see Philippians 4:8) rather than on any worldly cares and concerns.

A consecrated people will experience a purging of activities in their lives; many things will be cut away—things that may have been good but not spiritually profitable or fruit-producing. God will free us from the distractions and entanglements that have kept us from fully pursuing Him.

We can no longer afford to waste our energy on pursuits that do not really matter and are not truly profitable.

How do we use our time? Do we lavish it on ourselves, or do we lavish it on others through the service of our lives and resources? Stewardship of time, too, has been consecrated to the Lord. The Sabbath, a period of rest, is observed in the life of such a believer because it is a weekly reminder that our lives are not our own and that all we have is truly His.

Our finances are an investment into our life passions. The life marked by the Lord's name is truly humble and servantlike—a life that does not spend money selfishly, but freely invests in others. This lifestyle understands **"it is more blessed to give than to receive" (Acts 20:35)** and depicts godly wisdom and understanding in which finances are used to advance God's kingdom. This is a life that implements the law of the harvest and is not bound by a spirit of poverty.

God is not merely looking for people who are obedient, but rather He is seeking people who are *submissive* to His will. God is looking for willing vessels He can trust to put His name upon.

The Mark of His Presence

But you shall seek the place where the LORD your God chooses, out of all your tribes, to put His name for His dwelling place...(Deuteronomy 12:5).

My friend Bob Jones once said, "Where God puts His name, His Presence abides." When God puts His name on us, His Presence will live with us continually.

We will not merely visit His Presence at certain moments in our week, but His Presence will remain in us. Where we go, He will go.

God is not merely looking for people who are obedient, but rather He is seeking people who are *submissive* to His will.

There are many ways of telling if a person has been marked by the Presence of God:

- In the Lord's Presence is **"fullness of joy" (Psalm 16:11).**
- Set free from anxieties and fears, this person will be governed by peace (see John 14:27).
- Love is the distinguishing mark on this person (see Matthew 5:44).
- In Jesus, this person is made a light that illumines dark places (see Matthew 5:14).
- This person will bear the hope of His Presence (see Romans 5:1–2).
- He or she will discover Jesus as the One who heals all sickness (see Exodus 15:26). God's Presence always results in healing: spirit, soul, and body.
- Such believers will bear the Holy Spirit's fruit: love, joy, peace, longsuffering, kindness, goodness, faithfulness, gentleness, and self-control (see Galatians 5:22–23).

There are many other descriptions I could list of those who are marked by the Lord's Presence. Those who are *branded* by the Lord's name will manifest an amazing quality of life—a life filled with God's Presence.

The Mark of Authority

Authority can be inherited along the lines of a name, because a person's name includes the authority associated with that person's position and place. If we are marked by the name of the Lord, we will bear the authority intrinsic to His Presence. This, however, brings up an issue with the use of the Lord's name.

Often we have heard people passionately praying for things from God. They fervently pray and at the end of uttering all their requests, they simply say, "In Jesus' name." Sadly, sometimes such zealous ones do not maintain a lifestyle that reflects Christ's character. They have inadvertently reduced the Lord's name to a kind of lucky rabbit's foot. However, when a believer's life reflects the character of Jesus, that person's life is able to lay hold of God's authority. The source of authority is not merely in the name but in the character represented by the name. If we are marked by the Lord's name, then we will also be marked by the character and authority of Jesus.

The Mark of Humility and Brokenness

The apostle James wrote that "...**God resists the proud, but gives grace to the humble" (James 4:6).** Jesus was the ultimate Servant; the Gospels say He was meek and lowly of heart (see Matthew 11:29).

Those who are marked by the name of God have embraced the value of humility and have discovered the mystery of God's grace. Grace speaks of God's supernatural endowment to help us be what we are not, and to do what we cannot. Those who are humble shall be great in the kingdom because they have learned to keep themselves within the scope of God's work. They have learned to deny themselves in order to serve Christ more fully.

Jesus Himself spoke of the value of the humble in His Sermon on the Mount: **"Blessed are the poor in spirit, for theirs is the kingdom of heaven" (Matthew 5:3).** One of the greatest dangers in God's kingdom is the sin of spiritual pride. Those who wear the mark of humility find a potent shield of protection against this vice. Such people no longer worry about having to prove anything to anyone—they are totally secure in the Father's love and acceptance. They bear the mark of humility because they bear God's name.

Why is it important to list these components of a life marked by the name of the Lord? Because God's names are at stake in us; people will see God through the manifestation of His names in our lifestyles.

What an amazing God we serve! How could anyone ever want anything more than the gift of His name? Remember what King David sang:

> **Some boast in chariots, and some in horses, but we will boast in the name of the LORD, our God (Psalm 20:7 NAS).**

In Hebrew, the phrase to **"boast in"** means "to have confidence in, to trust in." Boasting in God's name indicates that we have confidence in His character, His attributes, and His nature—who He is.

God longs to free us from our sinful tendencies of doubt and self-promotion and our habit of trying to draw our confidence from our own resources or those of the people around us. This is the way of the world, but God's way is different.

God offers us a level of confidence and assurance that far surpasses any confidence the world could ever know. The world's confidence can be shaken because ultimately it is dependent upon human strength. The confidence God wants to give is never-ending; it cannot be disappointed; it cannot falter; it cannot fail because it is rooted in the very foundation of God's sovereign Presence, character, and nature. It is rooted in the unshakable foundation of His hallowed name!

God is extending the fullness of His name to you today. He is offering to put His name on you and give you *every* blessing that comes with it. How will you respond? Are you ready for the fire of preparation necessary for all who desire to receive His name?

For further reflection, ponder these questions before God:

1. Where do your affections lie?
2. What consumes your thoughts?
3. Do your actions glorify God or satisfy your own personal desires?
4. Do you do things that steal your time away from God?
5. Which characteristic listed in the Beatitudes (see Matthew 5:3–11) would you most like to flourish in your life?

As you embark on the adventure of knowing God, let Him show you the amazing mystery and wonder reserved for those who have chosen to receive and bear His name. Truly His name is above all names! ■

Adapted from *I AM: Inheriting the Fullness of God's Names* by John Paul Jackson. Copyright 2004. Used by permission. For more information, visit www.streamsministries.com.

To our condemnation we confess that this rush age is molding our living, whereas we should mold the age.

—Leonard Ravenhill

Mustard Seeds of Wisdom

The GREAT LIBERATION

by Rick Joyner

O ne of the most controversial doctrines throughout the church age has been the place of women in the church, especially whether they should be allowed to teach or exercise authority in the church. This is no small matter, and must be settled before we can come into our full purpose as the church. When it is settled, it will release one of the greatest overall advances in the church since the giving of the Holy Spirit.

Like any true doctrinal resolution, this must be done without compromising the Scriptures, but rather basing our doctrine on them, rightly dividing the written Word that has been given to us for that purpose. In this article, I intend to agitate two major controversies, not for the purpose of creating more division, but so these issues are confronted until they are resolved.

First, it is my position, which I will base on Scripture, that women must not only be allowed to teach in the church, but that a great and crucial teaching ministry has been deposited by God in women. It is also my position that there should be no ceiling on the authority that a woman can exercise in the church, including apostolic authority, which is also established in the Scriptures.

Second, it is also my position, based on studies and observation, that the church has become so feminine that most men feel uncomfortable or bored. Even though the majority of the church is presently led by men, about 75 percent of the church are women who want their husbands, sons, and brothers to be attracted to the church. In general, this will not happen until there is a place for the masculine nature in the church.

How could the church, which is so predominantly led by men, have such a tendency to make the church overly feminine? To some degree, this is a result of the devil's overwhelming assault to blur the distinctions between men and women. It is also, at least partially, the result of women exercising illegal influence over the church because they have not been allowed to do it legally.

> **True men are never intimidated by true women, and true women are never intimidated by true men.**

This is not to imply that there should not be feminine influence in the church, and even a feminine identity. In fact, I believe there should be even more than there is now, but it should not exclude the masculine. We should have both. This, too, must be corrected for the church to come into its full purpose.

The church should be the foremost place on earth where men are free to be men, women are free to be women, and everyone is completely free to be who God created them to be, using all of their gifts and talents for His glory. Such a place would be one of the most attractive societies to all people on the earth, which is why the devil is so intent on blurring the distinctions that God made between men and women.

True men are never intimidated by true women, and true women are never intimidated by true men. When both are real about who they are, they set others free to be who they are. It is actually the wrongful compromises that are causing the divisions because anyone who is compromising who they truly are will always be insecure. One of the greatest revolutions in Christianity is about to come because the Lord is going to set the men free to be who He created them to be, and He is going to set the women free to be who He created them to be.

The Great Teaching Ministry

It is basic to Christianity to understand that the Lord came to give us life and to give it more abundantly. Life is our primary business. The word "father" means "life-giver" because the sperm seed of life comes from the man. However, let us think for a minute. What would happen to that seed if there was no woman present? Who is it that carries the seed, nurtures it, brings forth the life, and does the biggest part of the job of raising that life to maturity? Basically, until the child is born men do the fun part and the women do all the work. After the child is born, and through its most important formative years, the mother will usually continue to be the greatest source of nurture and teaching.

I am not advocating changing this. In fact, it is, I believe, a divine order of things. However, I do advocate giving honor to whom honor is due. I believe motherhood is possibly the highest calling that one can have on this earth. Every mother is a "queen mother," and should be treated like one and given the highest place of dignity and respect.

A Prophetic Experience

The next three paragraphs came from a prophetic experience. I do not believe prophecy should be used to establish doctrine in the church; only the written Word of God can be used for that. I am not trying to establish a doctrine here by sharing this prophetic experience, but I am sharing how I came to the following conclusions. Prophecy is sometimes given to illuminate doctrine and illuminate the Scriptures, but if we do not see it in the written Word it should not be accepted. I was given these prophetic experiences in order to see where the true spiritual authority often comes from and how much more we should be devoted to prayer and to honoring, even celebrating, mothers on the earth. In this I am speaking of both natural and spiritual mothers.

I have had several prophetic experiences in which I was standing before the throne of the Lord in heaven. In two of them I was able to observe that many, if not a majority, of those who were close to the Lord's throne were women. There are things in such experiences that you just know you are supposed to see or understand; I knew that most of these were mother intercessors who were the ones truly responsible for some of the great moves of God upon the earth. Most of these moves were led by men, who are known for them on the earth, but in heaven these women were known for them. They were the ones who carried the spiritual seed, nurtured and protected it until it matured.

It was then that I began to understand that many who are the most well-known on earth are not well-known in heaven, and many who are not well-known on earth are some of the most well-known in heaven. The hidden ministry of the intercessor was intended to be hidden, even in Scripture, until the day of judgment. In fact, this ministry loses its power when it becomes too well-known on the earth. However, those who "see" should recognize where true authority comes from. Having authority with God is much more important than having authority with men.

> I knew that most of these were mother intercessors who were the ones truly responsible for some of the great moves of God upon the earth.

After these experiences I started to believe that when John and Andrew came to Jesus and asked to sit at His right hand and left, He could not grant this because it was reserved. Many of those for whom it was prepared are women. Prayer can have more authority on the earth than the United Nations and all other seats of authority combined. For the most part, women have chosen this "best part" far more often than men.

Even so, the Lord is about to display true womanhood in all of its glory through the church. This will compel women to see and understand all that they were created to be. The Lord is also about to display true manhood in all of its glory and all that it is called to be through the church. This, too, will cause all men to understand who they were created to be. This will also make it possible for both men and women to accept and respect the place of the other. This world was not made to be either masculine or feminine, but the place where both could thrive as they were created.

Could there be a ministry more worthy of honor and support than the ministry of being a mother?

It is also in this that true unity will come. The way I become one with my wife is not by making her into a man, but by honoring and appreciating her differences, seeing them as complimentary, not conflicting. Now let's look at the teaching ministry God has given to women, and how essential it is to a healthy church life. Then we will address the authority issue.

The Great Calling

In Proverbs 6:20-23 we read:

My son, observe the commandment of your father, and do not forsake the teaching of your mother;

Bind them continually on your heart; tie them around your neck.

When you walk about, they will guide you; when you sleep, they will watch over you; and when you awake, they will talk to you.

For the commandment is a lamp, and the teaching is light; and reproofs for discipline are the way of life.

Here we are told to observe the commandments of our fathers, and not forsake the *teachings* of our mothers. It is said that our basic character traits are set by the time we are four years old. Therefore, this is when teaching and instruction are the most critical. The mother's teaching has its greatest impact on the child during these most formative years, and this can have the greatest impact on the course of a person's life. Is there any teaching ministry more important than this? Could there be a ministry more worthy of honor and support than the ministry of being a mother?

In Exodus 20:12 we read the commandment to: **"Honor your father and your mother, that your days may be prolonged in the land which the Lord your God gives you."** In Ephesians 6:1-3, Paul restates this commandment, ensuring that it would receive the same compliance by those under the New Covenant: **"Children, obey your parents in the Lord, for this is right. Honor your father and mother (which is the first commandment with a promise), that it may be well with you, and that you may live long on the earth."** All of the commandments reveal God's standards for righteousness. Except for the ones commanding us to love, the commandment to honor our fathers and mothers is emphasized more in both the New and Old Testaments than all of the others. As Paul pointed out, this is actually the only commandment with a promise attached, and that promise is longevity.

The church has done a fair job of honoring spiritual fathers, but having been a Christian for almost thirty-five years now, I have not heard spiritual mothers even mentioned more than a couple of times. The commandment is that we honor both, yet I do not believe that much of the church even understands what a spiritual mother is. A good case can be made that the primary reason why so many churches and movements become spiritually irrelevant so fast, not having longevity, is because they do not honor both. If we are going to be the church that we have been called to be, we must recognize and honor both our spiritual fathers and mothers.

I confess to having a deep and growing love for Catholics, while at the same time having a great and deep grief for many of their doctrines and practices. The one that I especially consider an extreme is the degree to which the veneration of Mary has been taken. This was seared in my heart when I walked into the great cathedral in Cologne, Germany, and saw what I estimated to be more than a thousand candles burning under the picture of Mary, but just one flickering little candle burning under the picture of Jesus! However, I also think that Protestants and Evangelicals do not honor Mary, the mother of Jesus, enough, even though we are told in Scripture that she was to be honored so that all generations would call her blessed (see Luke 1:48). Maybe this is an overreaction to Catholic practices, but both are extremes.

> **If we are going to be the church that we have been called to be, we must recognize and honor both our spiritual fathers and mothers.**

Certainly that young girl who risked all that she did to carry and give birth to the Son of God is deserving of being considered one of the greatest heroes of the faith for all time. However, she did not just carry the seed of the Holy Spirit and give birth to the Son of God, but persevered with Him through the cross, and remained faithful to Him until the end, even when all but one of His apostles had fled in fear.

Though I consider it the most anointed movie ever made, I could hardly endure watching Mel Gibson's movie, *The Passion of the Christ*. Even knowing that it was a movie, and knowing that they were all actors, it was still almost unbearable to watch a portrayal of our King being tortured the way that He was. Yet Mary stood by her Son, beholding the real torture and crucifixion, which lasted many more hours than the movie, and she stayed with Him until the very end. Why? Because she was a mother.

> **Most of the great men and women of God can point to their mothers, like Solomon did, as the real reason behind their success.**

Mary is worthy of honor, not worship, and maybe more than any other person in the Gospels except her Son. God has deposited faithfulness and faith into motherhood, and it deserves such honor. However, we must now ask: How is it that Catholics would go to such extremes in honoring Mary, and not even allow women to be priests? This seems remarkably incongruous, but there are similar contradictions in the practices of much of the rest of the church concerning the place of women.

This is a matter that must be addressed and rectified if we are going to fulfill our full purpose. This is why Paul reminded Timothy that it was because of his mother and grandmother that he was in the faith (see II Timothy 1:5). We will also see how Paul, contrary to what many assert, gave such honor to women, their teaching ministry, and their authority. We will do this without in any way bending the Scriptures, but we will have to straighten out a few wrong interpretations, which are easily revealed as such.

Who Is the Priest?

This leads to another issue. There was a doctrine promulgated in the 1970s that the man was "the priest of the home." I felt at the time that this would be a devastating doctrine in the church, and I think we can see clearly now just how devastating it was. As stated, Timothy's mother and grandmother were responsible for him being in the faith. Most of the great men and women of God can point to their mothers, like Solomon did, as the real reason behind their success.

First, all Christians are called to be priests, not just men. This doctrine seemed to be an attempt to instill the importance of men being the spiritual heads of their homes, but it was very misguided. Priests are intercessors, and the fact is that, in general, women tend to be much better intercessors than men, and because of this doctrine, some of the best intercessors were neutralized.

Many people like to point to the failures of highly visible ministries during the 1980s as the reason for the great slide of moral integrity in the church, but I think at least a good part of this can be traced to some of the doctrines in the 1970s that took prayer, one of our greatest weapons, out of the hands of many who knew best how to use it.

If this doctrine was taken from the Old Covenant, the perpetrators should have followed the model to its conclusion. There was a division of authority between the kings and priests under the Old Covenant. The kings held secular authority in order to allow the priests to be devoted to the divine service and to teach the ways of the Lord to the people. Likewise, in the New Testament the man is the head of the home, but this is in order to take care of the management of the affairs so that the woman can be free to do that which is more important. In the Lord, those in authority are the servants of those under them.

What women are called to do in the home, in intercession, and teaching the children, is far more important than going out and making money. If we look at it from a worldly, human perspective in these times, in a society that scores value so much according to possessions and wealth, it is understandable why women staying at home with the children might think of themselves as second-class citizens. However, this will not be the case for anyone looking from the more important, spiritual perspective.

I personally have no trouble with women having careers and professions, and believe that they should be rewarded with both money and authority commensurate with their accomplishments, equal to men who do the same things, but that is a low calling, not the high calling that motherhood is. Even so, the real issue is: Are we doing the Lord's will? I have no doubt that many women are doing the Lord's will in the profession, but I also have no doubt that many, who may still be doing a great job and accomplishing much, have settled for less than they could have attained in this life by not esteeming their calling as mothers far above any secular profession. It is what we do for eternity that really counts. Many of the accomplishments that may have received the accolades of men will look very shallow on the Day of Judgment. The real issue is whether we were seeking first the kingdom of heaven in our pursuits, or our own interests.

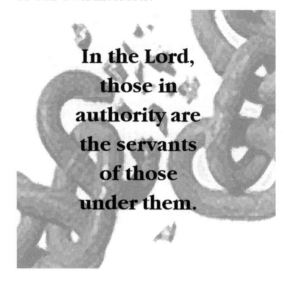

In the Lord, those in authority are the servants of those under them.

The Greatest Wisdom

King Solomon was said to be the wisest man who ever lived, except of course for the Lord Jesus. After writing the book of Proverbs, which is the only book in the Bible devoted exclusively to wisdom, Solomon concluded it was: **"...the oracle which his mother taught him" (Proverbs 31:1).** The wisest man who ever ruled on earth was taught his great wisdom by his mother!

Solomon's mother knew that he was destined to be king, and she saw and devoted herself to preparing him for his destiny. It was an awesome calling to prepare the future king, but our children have a greater calling than Solomon; they are called to rule and reign with Christ. Therefore, every mother of a Christian child is a true "queen mother" who deserves even more honor than any queen mother of a mere earthly kingdom.

It is probably the intercession of mothers, in the natural and spiritual, that enable more people to assume their callings and purposes...

The following statement by Solomon in the Song of Solomon is also quite enlightening:

Go forth, O daughters of Zion, and gaze on King Solomon with the crown with which his mother has crowned him on the day of his wedding, and on the day of his gladness of heart (Song of Solomon 3:11).

Solomon was the son of David, the greatest king of Israel. He was the heir to the throne because of his father, yet here he confesses that it was his mother who crowned him.

If we read the story in Scripture, we see that one of Solomon's brothers was trying to seize the crown for himself when Solomon's mother went and interceded for her son with King David, and Solomon was then crowned. Likewise, it is probably the intercession of mothers, in the natural and spiritual, that enable more people to assume their callings and purposes than we will probably ever suspect until it is revealed to all on the Day of Judgment.

Again, we need to consider why there has been so much attention given to honoring spiritual fathers, but so little to spiritual mothers. It is probably because so much of that ministry is hidden, carried out in prayer before the Lord. Such ministry is still not esteemed in the church the way that it should be.

Some may have the argument that Solomon ended up falling, so his foundation must not have been as strong as it should have been. That is true, but I do not think it was because he honored his mother too much, or did not honor his father enough. The fact is Solomon did have longevity and was allowed to remain king for many years after he introduced apostasies into the nation. An argument could be made that this was actually the result of him honoring his father too much. By this I mean that Solomon only had his father's vision and when he finished building the house of the Lord, he did not have a vision of his own, so he drifted from the faith.

To truly honor our fathers and mothers does not mean that we cannot go farther than they did, or have a vision for things that they may not have had. In fact, if you listen to a truly loving father or mother, they delight in seeing their children go farther than they did. Our ceiling should be the floor of the next generation. The way they can honor us most is by taking what we leave to them and going much further.

The Lord Is Masculine

Another issue that must be settled is the fact that the Lord is masculine. Again, one of the devil's ultimate intentions to thwart the purpose of God is to blur the distinctions that God made between men and women. One of the ultimate conclusions and delusions of this apostasy is to try to make God into a woman. It is not "our mother in heaven," He is our Father in heaven. He did not create us Adam and Steve, but Adam and Eve. Jesus was a man and is *the man* Christ Jesus. As the Scripture makes clear, He continues to be the One as the mediator between God and man (see I Timothy 2:5). This cannot be compromised, and those who try to erode this clear teaching of Scripture are on the path to a profound deception and bondage, not liberty.

It is the delusion of the pretenders to true authority, who obviously know of their own inadequacy, to suppose that for them to ascend to their purpose they have to bring others lower. No true woman, who is confident in her own purpose, is in any way intimidated or offended by God being masculine or by any man being masculine. It is only the weak, insecure, or deceived who think that for them to advance they have to change others, or anything external for that matter.

Let us also consider this—the Lord is so secure in who He is that He is not intimidated by His bride, the church, doing even greater works than He did. In fact, He wants her to. Likewise, no true man who is secure in his manhood is intimidated by his wife doing even greater things than he has done. In fact, a true man will applaud, support, and encourage her, just as the Lord does His bride.

The bride of Christ may do greater works than the Lord did while on the earth, but she will do it through His power and authority. Likewise, every husband and wife team is a partnership. However, some of the great men of God and great men of faith are those who allow their wives to be all that they are called to be, and do all that they are called to do.

Women do not have to emasculate the men to be able to minister or take the authority that men are called to walk in, but rather the reverse is true—they need to find men who are men and who are secure enough to let them be who they were created to be. The only freedom that any of us will ever know is to be who God created us to be and allow others to do the same.

Women in Business

It is fitting that Solomon concludes his great book of wisdom, the book of Proverbs, with an entire chapter devoted to the perfect woman. It is also noteworthy that some of the most esteemed characteristics of this woman were her business skills. She was into real estate, developing, manufacturing, and was a remarkable manager. Her husband delighted in her for it.

If you want a New Testament reference, Lydia was a businesswoman in Phillipi, the first to receive the Word of God in Asia, and it was in her house that the disciples met (see Acts 16:14, 40). God has given to women some of the greatest gifts for business and management, and the truly wise men appreciate it, and not only free them to do it, but honor and appreciate them for it.

> **One thing we are committed to is basing our doctrines and practices on Scripture above all things.**

The Great Controversy

All of this brings up an important and controversial issue: What about the New Testament Scriptures that say women should not be allowed to teach or even speak in the church? That is a good question. One thing we are committed to is basing our doctrines and practices on Scripture above all things. First let us look at I Timothy 2:11-15:

> **Let a woman quietly receive instruction with entire submissiveness.**
>
> **But I do not allow a woman to teach or exercise authority over a man, but to remain quiet.**
>
> **For it was Adam who was first created, and then Eve.**
>
> **And it was not Adam who was deceived, but the woman being quite deceived, fell into transgression.**

> **But women shall be preserved through the bearing of children if they continue in faith and love and sanctity with self-restraint.**

Now let us consider that many have taken this statement as a conclusion that because Eve was deceived, women are more prone to deception than men. How many wars were started by women? How many cults, sects, or false teachings? How many false religions? Now answer these same questions about men. So do you still think women are more prone to deception than men? These obvious facts have made this an issue for many over the years. Then why would Paul say this? That is a question that deserves an answer. Even if this statement is true as intended, if only Eve was deceived, then Adam knew what he was doing! How smart was that?

Before addressing this let us look at I Corinthians 14:34-35, which says:

> **Let the women keep silent in the churches; for they are not permitted to speak, but let them subject themselves, just as the Law also says.**
>
> **And if they desire to learn anything, let them ask their own husbands at home; for it is improper for a woman to speak in church.**

These Scriptures are so clear and straightforward. How could we possibly doubt that this was exactly what the apostle meant? I will give you six reasons:

1) It is in contradiction to other Scriptures.
2) It is contrary to the entire weight of Scripture.

3) It is in contradiction to Paul's own practice.

4) Nowhere does the Law say this.

5) The fruit that has come from this interpretation is bad.

6) If we are to honor our mothers, what could possibly be more dishonoring than to tell them that they are not even able to speak in church?

The main reasons why these two verses have been challenged by sincere Bible-believing Christians is when they are taken literally, they stand in contradiction to other Scriptures, which cannot be overlooked. A basic principle of biblical interpretation is found in Psalm 119:160: **"The sum of Thy word is truth, and every one of Thy righteous ordinances is everlasting."** If there is ever an apparent contradiction in Scripture, there is a reason for it.

A basic principle of biblical interpretation is even if you do not understand the reason for such a seeming contradiction, you never base your doctrine on the one or two Scriptures that stand in contradiction to the rest of the Bible, but always go with the **"sum"** of the Word or the weight of Scripture. Even so, this does not justify overlooking any Scripture. If there is a seeming contradiction in Scripture, we can be assured it is intended to be there by God. The tension between seeming contradictions is meant to drive us to a deeper understanding. I say here "seeming" contradictions because even in those that seem the most apparent, I have learned there is always a higher perspective that will bring both into light and into harmony with each other, regardless of how impossible this may seem.

> **The tension between seeming contradictions is meant to drive us to a deeper understanding.**

Another problem that scholars and leaders of the church have had in literally interpreting these two verses is that nowhere in the Law does it say that women are not permitted to speak in the congregation. Paul, who had been the "Pharisee of Pharisees" would have known this better than anyone. This seems to confirm what theologians have asserted, that Paul was quoting here a letter or a report *from* the Corinthians concerning practices they had adopted and was replying to them. These consider the next verses to be Paul's reply to the Corinthian practice of not allowing women to speak:

Was it from you that the word of God first went forth? Or has it come to you only?

If anyone thinks he is a prophet or spiritual, let him recognize that the things which I write to you are the Lord's commandment.

But if anyone does not recognize this, he is not recognized.

Therefore, my brethren, desire earnestly to prophesy, and do not forbid to speak in tongues.

But let all things be done properly and in an orderly manner (I Corinthians 14:36-40).

> **Paul named Priscilla first, indicating by the clear protocol of the times that Priscilla was the preeminent one instructing Apollos.**

My wife and daughter recently visited the church in Corinth, Greece, and were given another interesting explanation for these verses. It was explained to them that many of the temple prostitutes had been converted in Corinth, and by custom, had their heads shaved. To protect them from more scorn in the church, Paul issued a decree for the church in Corinth that all women should wear head coverings. Also, because of the heated bickering between the women of the church and these converted temple prostitutes, Paul also mandated that all of the women should keep silent in the church. They asserted that this was only for the church in Corinth because of this special circumstance, which is why Paul did not mandate this practice in any other churches. It is true that none of the other churches in the New Testament were given this instruction or had this practice.

There have been many other interesting and sometimes convincing explanations given to these verses by some of the great teachers in history. Probably the best reason why these verses are not to be taken as a doctrine that Paul intended for the whole church is that it is in contradiction to Paul's own practice.

Paul acknowledges in Romans that Priscilla and Aquila instructed Apollos, who himself became one of the greatest teachers in the first century church. Paul named Priscilla first, indicating by the clear protocol of the times that Priscilla was the preeminent one instructing Apollos. It was even considered in the first century to have been an intentional statement of liberation for women in the church to teach men. Paul further established this at the end of this letter to the Romans. When he listed those that the church in Rome should greet, Priscilla was again named first as if to verify his intention in this (see Romans 16:3).

In Romans 16:7 Paul writes, **"Greet Andronicus and Junias, my kinsmen, and my fellow prisoners, who are outstanding among the apostles, who also were in Christ before me."** This clearly names a woman among the apostles. We are also told that the apostolic office was given to be a "witness of the resurrection" (see Acts 1:22, 4:33).

It is noteworthy that the very first witness of the Lord's resurrection was a woman. She actually bore witness of it to the apostles, who were at the time cowering in fear and did not believe the witness!

Obviously it takes far more bending of Scripture to hold to the doctrine that women should not be allowed to speak in church, or have authority, than it does to accept that they should. However, both positions or conclusions can leave unanswered questions for those who are sincere seekers of truth and genuinely desire to obey the Word of God. I, therefore, do not believe that either position should be held so dogmatically that we allow it to divide us. We must so esteem the Scriptures that we would never rationalize a text we do not agree with. Having heard and read a multitude of teachings on this subject, and having examined it myself, I base my doctrine and practice on what I consider to be the weight of the Scriptures rather than a single text that seems in contradiction to it, while remaining tolerant of those who see it otherwise.

There are many other ways in which both the Lord and the apostles honored and elevated the status of women in bold departures from the practice of the times. As stated, the Lord chose a woman to be the first to see and declare His resurrection, which was in fact the apostolic mandate. As He promised in Psalm 68:11, **"The Lord gives the command; the women who proclaim the good tidings are a great host."** Without question, some of the greatest evangelists in history have been women, and some of the greatest today, who I think merit being considered true apostles, are women.

A third major, theological problem of not allowing women to speak in the church is that we have women named as prophetesses in both the Old and New Testaments. This includes Miriam and Deborah in the Old Testament (see Exodus 15:20, Judges 4:4) and Anna and Philip's daughters in the New Testament (see Acts 21:9). We are also told in the books of Joel and Acts that when the Lord pours out His Spirit, our sons and daughters will prophesy (see Joel 2:29). Would God give someone the gift of prophecy, but not allow them to speak?

> **I base my doctrine and practice on what I consider to be the weight of the Scriptures rather than a single text**

It should also be noted that just before Paul seemingly mandated in his letter to the Corinthians that women should not be allowed to speak, he wrote that if they prophesied, they should do so with their head covered. How could they prophesy if they could not speak?

Another major problem that we have if we do not allow women to teach or speak in the church may be the most important of all. Could there be anything more dishonoring to our mothers than to tell them that they are not even allowed to speak in church? These are the ones who have probably been our most important teachers. These are the ones who not only gave life to us, but nurtured and taught us from the beginning. The Lord thought it was so important for us to honor them that it is the only commandment He gave with a promise attached to it—the promise of long life, which to most would be one of the greatest promises of all.

> **We must rise up and preempt the enemy by taking the high ground on every important issue of our times.**

Summary

We will be limited in our spiritual advancement until this matter is resolved in the church. This involves more than half of the present citizens of the kingdom, more than half of the members of the body of Christ. Until women are allowed to function in the place to which they have been called, the body of Christ will be at best like a stroke victim that is half paralyzed.

The church is called to be the light of the world. This implies that we must have the answers to the world's pressing problems. **"Where the Spirit of the Lord is there is liberty" (II Corinthians 3:17).** Yet the church in our times has not only failed to lead the great liberation movements of recent times, we have often been their greatest enemies. This must change.

When we fail to lead with sound biblical truth, the enemy will fill the vacuum with every form of perversion. Many leaders in the church have mistaken the nature of those who filled the vacuum as the nature of the whole movement. The primary reason why there are such perversions and extremes in the women's liberation movement is because the church did not take the lead in setting women free from the oppression they had been subject to. This movement should not have to be led by women; godly men who have the heart of God for His children and household should have led it long ago!

We must rise up and preempt the enemy by taking the high ground on every important issue of our times. Even if we are starting late, as much of the church is doing in relation to women's liberation, it is not too late to seize the high ground of sound biblical truth, take our stand, and push the darkness back.

One of the great problems that we have in the church today is that there are many teachers, but not many fathers. Most whom I have heard described as spiritual fathers are older men who have served faithfully for many years, and are not spiritual fathers, but just old teachers. A father is not just someone who is old, but someone who reproduces. Most men become fathers when they are young, not old. A spiritual father is someone who reproduces his ministry and the grace that he has been given in others. However, for a man to become a father, there must be a woman present. For a man to become a father, a woman must also become a mother. We must start recognizing and honoring both our spiritual fathers and mothers.

We need to recognize and honor the women who carry the seed of the Lord through intercession, and then nurture the young with words of life and a constant vigilance. These spiritual mothers will be some of the best teachers of newborn believers, just as mothers are the best teachers of young children. This is not to negate the place of the men in this, but God made men and women to be different and did divide the labor required to propagate the race. This does not negate the place of women teaching on the highest or more advanced levels either, but the foundations are more important to lay properly. This is a great gift and honor that the Lord has given especially to women.

When the world sees godly women of the church in their God-given roles, being fulfilled to the uttermost because they are being who they were called to be, motherhood and womanhood will be esteemed as the glorious callings that they are.

The Lord wants to display womanhood just as He wants to display His bride, the church. The church is a bride, and is referred to in the feminine because that is the nature she is called to reveal. The church will never be able to do this without women being in their place.

> **We need to recognize and honor the women who carry the seed of the Lord through intercession, and then nurture the young with words of life and a constant vigilance.**

We also need to understand that the bride is to be like "an army with banners," which is quite masculine, and we will not be that until men are in their place. These may seem to be contradictory natures, but the male and female natures perfectly compliment one another when they are right. When the Lord is finished with His church, the world will see in it the perfect glory of both the man and the woman. Men will look at the men in the church and say, "That is what I am called to be." Women will look at the women in the church and say, "That is what I am called to be." True unity will only come when men are men and women are allowed to be women. There would be no Jezebels if there were no Ahabs. Until we are both free, neither can be free. ∎

Humble HEART

by Sally Boenau

Jesus, You have given me a most
    important part—
A sharing of Your precious yoke—
    a meek and humble heart.
The rage of all that's worldly in my
    thought and word and deed
Cannot destroy Your living Words—
    Your incorruptible seed.

A union of our spirits, an adoption
    of my soul,
An ever-increasing knowing of just
    how You make me whole.
Jesus, how surprised I am to find
    what makes for life—
What God must cut away of me with
    His ever-living knife.

The pain, the strain, conflicting thought
    of what is really right;
The shame, the blame one must endure
    to exercise new sight.
When passion and my indignation
    explode at what's unfair,
And standing firm and loving are the
    things I can hardly bear,
I think of You and how You felt when
    You were in a garden,
And how your path through darkest
    night was one that led to pardon.

Oh thank You, thank You faithful
    Witness, for showing me the way—
Humbleness of heart and mind will
    be my choice this day.

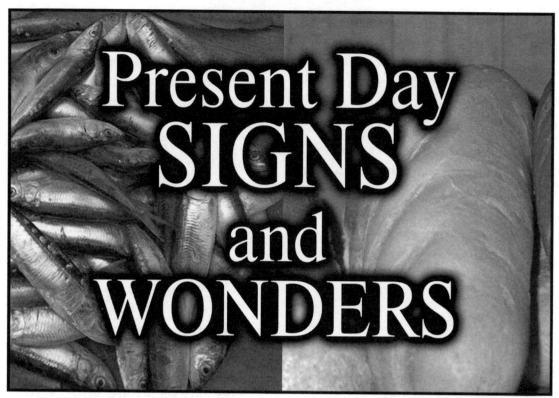

Present Day SIGNS and WONDERS

by Paul Keith Davis

A. W. Tozer said it best with the title of his classic book, *The Pursuit of God*. The ultimate adventure for this generation is the pursuit of the Lord Jesus Christ. There can be no greater endeavor than to know Him as personally as He may be known. The Scripture promises, if we draw near to Him, He will draw near to us.

The "one thing" that characterized King David's life was his hungry heart. David loved the Lord's presence more than anything else, and for that the Lord loved and trusted him (see James 4:8). Devotion to becoming God's "friend" is our most noble pilgrimage (see John 15:15).

Even so, we are also given clear and concise biblical affirmations of the functioning of His victorious church. There is a mandate placed upon the latter-day church to gather the harvest and awaken a misguided generation to its righteous destiny. To accomplish this mandate, we must be endowed with heaven's virtue and empowered with the overcoming victory of the Lord's redemptive work. The Lord's example and demonstration of mighty works are necessary for this inevitable responsibility, and as He promised, even greater works (see John 14:12).

The gospel of the kingdom is the power of God leading to salvation. This gospel does not merely consist in Words, but also in God's sovereign power. The ministry of signs and wonders does not diminish the supernatural nature of God's written Word; it confirms it.

God's revealed Word is plainly established by the Holy Spirit's endorsement. He demonstrates approval or affirmation through signs, wonders, and manifestations of the Spirit.

According to the writer of Hebrews, the Lord's Spirit works with His people by: **testifying with them, both by signs and wonders and by various miracles and by gifts of the Holy Spirit according to His own will (Hebrews 2:4).**

> **There must be a balance in our personal endeavor to know the Lord and our mandate to win this generation through the Spirit's demonstration of power.**

God's power and witness are fundamentally necessary for us to accomplish heaven's blueprint. We simply do not posses the ability within ourselves to accomplish God's ultimate plan. We need God and the embodiment of His Spirit that provides power. Even so, as wonderful and necessary as incredible displays of the Spirit are, we cannot allow them to supersede our quest to know Him as the Living Word.

A Word of Wisdom

John G. Lake was a man used powerfully as a missionary to South Africa and healing evangelist throughout America. History now documents wonderful miracles and spiritual wonders that the Lord performed through this humble servant. Nevertheless, in 1925 he discerned that his generation "missed the mark" by being more captured by the phenomena of God than the Person. The same was true in the days of Moses when he said:

> **You have seen all that the LORD did before your eyes in the land of Egypt to Pharaoh and all his servants and all his land;**
>
> **the great trials which your eyes have seen, those great signs and wonders.**
>
> **Yet to this day the LORD has not given you a heart to know, nor eyes to see, nor ears to hear (Deuteronomy 29:2-4).**

Consequently, there must be a balance in our personal endeavor to know the Lord and our mandate to win this generation through the Spirit's demonstration of power. Through fellowship with Him, our spiritual senses become keenly sensitive to His voice and the message being confirmed through signs and wonders. These prerogatives must be maintained in the proper biblical order.

The Original Model

The ministry of the early church was profound on many levels. By natural standards, the credentials of the individuals utilized were not impressive.

For the most part, their personal abilities left them unqualified for their pioneering assignment. Even so, they received an impartation from God that validated their mission and facilitated the revelation of God's kingdom. They believed God and trusted not in their own strength, but in His.

The Bible plainly outlines the many signs and miraculous wonders that accompanied the early church in their task. The Scripture tells us that reverential awe fell upon many as miraculous wonders took place. People were added to the church daily and God's name was notably glorified (see Acts 2:41-43).

These are the same results we need today. Our task is no less important or difficult than the one given to the early apostolic church. In fact, in many ways ours is even more intense. Therefore, we need all that the early church had and in multiplied fashion.

The early disciples preached the gospel of the kingdom and ministered to people's spirits, souls, and bodies. They did not "shrink from declaring the whole purpose of God" (see Acts 20:27).

Furthermore, in the midst of persecution and an unbelieving generation, their message was confirmed with the Holy Spirit's power imparted to them on the Day of Pentecost. It was their prayer that the Lord would:

...grant to Your servants that with all boldness they may speak Your word,

by stretching out Your hand to heal, and that signs and wonders may be done through the name of Your holy Servant Jesus (Acts 4:29-30 NKJV).

God's power is a witness to the gospel. That is why the early church passionately prayed to be empowered with signs and wonders as an instrument to convey the good news of the kingdom and win the lost.

> **The early disciples preached the gospel of the kingdom and ministered to people's spirits, souls, and bodies.**

A Twentieth Century Token

In each expression of spiritual outpouring throughout church history, God's presence was authenticated with various expressions of His Spirit. During the early twentieth century, Maria Woodworth-Etter's ministry was characterized by wonderful manifestations of spiritual signs and miraculous wonders like those done by the early apostolic believers. Marvelous displays of healing and deliverance were prevalent in her meetings. Additionally, it was not uncommon for many people to "fall under the power" and remain in that condition for many days. The Bible promised to "bear witness" to the kingdom message with diverse and various miracles and gifts of the Holy Spirit (see Hebrews 2:4).

We are promised a visitation of God's presence to awaken the church to her end-time responsibility and influence.

Oftentimes doctors would examine the people while in this condition to determine their heart rate and other vital statistics. In each case it was reported that every individual was in a perfectly healthy state. They were overshadowed with God's Spirit and prostrate before God without food, water, or movement. It was reported that in some cases people remained in this condition for as long as seven days. This was confirmed by both the secular and Christian media.

Tremendous testimonies of healing, deliverance, and divine commissions were reported following the encounters. During these experiences it was well-documented that many people would be commissioned to foreign lands and come out of the experience able to fluently speak the language of the nation to which they were sent. Furthermore, many accounts report the spirit of conviction that accompanied these manifestations to such an extent that the most hardened characters melted into weeping repentance.

This was a token of the heritage of God's people and the empowerment of His presence essential in the fulfillment of our latter-day mandate.

A Present Sign and Wonder

There exists an elevated atmosphere of anticipation and encouragement for this generation to experience profound expressions of God's power. We are promised a visitation of God's presence to awaken the church to her end-time responsibility and influence. We are now beginning to see more evidence of this in the Western church. God's strategic plan is unfolding at an escalated pace.

This past February, David and Donna Kelly hosted a conference in Cincinnati, Ohio. Wanda and I joined Rick Joyner, James Goll, and Patricia King as the speakers. At this conference the Lord granted a wonderful affirmation. It was indeed a sign and a wonder that has generated fruitful results and mobilized faith in countless believers. The theme was "Engaging Heaven." It has been the quest of many individuals and fellowships to be awakened with acute spiritual eyes and ears that provide hearts of understanding and cooperation with heaven. During the conference, the Lord's Spirit provided specific endorsement to the importance of this theme and its current relevance.

According to Proverbs 29:18: **"where there is no vision, the people are unrestrained"** and perish. This phrase conveys the necessity for the spirit of revelation to exist in God's people in order for there to be advancement. The Hebrew word used for **"vision"** implies "open vision" for communicating God's heart and strategic design. Revelation provides spiritual eyes that see and ears that hear, thereby facilitating hearts with comprehension.

On the first evening of the conference, the host pastors, along with numerous other workers, friends, and technicians visibly saw and spoke with an individual whom they have known for years. This brother is an itinerant minister from Nashville who had planned to attend the conference. The people at the registration desk assisted him with his name badge and conference information. Also, several people spoke with him on the opening evening of the conference, and most said that his short response was merely a word or blessing. The interesting thing is, this brother was in Nashville, Tennessee at the time these appearances occurred.

An Extraordinary Appearance

Weeks earlier, the Kelly's leadership team and intercessory base felt compelled to initiate a forty day fast leading up to the conference. There seemed to be a weightiness associated with heaven's mandate for the gathering. The Holy Spirit encouraged them by releasing a prophetic word expressing His desire to deeply impact the attendees and the region's spiritual atmosphere. The battles have been long and wearisome, but these prophetic messages of hope and destiny provide encouragement to leadership and the Lord's body. The Lord is granting wonderful tokens of confidence to position us for our spiritual release.

> **Revelation provides spiritual eyes that see and ears that hear, thereby facilitating hearts with comprehension.**

The decreed fast ended on February 16 and the conference began on Thursday, February 17. During the opening evening, someone with the identical appearance of the brother from Nashville was clearly seen in the balcony. The host pastors acknowledged his presence during the opening session prompting others in the balcony to embrace and greet him.

The following morning, February 18, this brother came to the meetings, but disclosed that he had departed Nashville at 2 a.m. in order to arrive in time for the morning session. Naturally, the Kelly's attempted to correct this and acknowledged that he was actually in the service the previous evening. He had been publicly acknowledged and greeted by many friends.

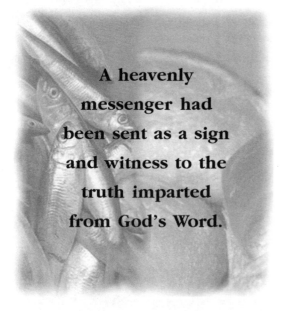

A heavenly messenger had been sent as a sign and witness to the truth imparted from God's Word.

Surprised at their insistence, he adamantly denied being in the service the previous evening. He had been in a fellowship gathering in Nashville with other believers until 11 p.m. This fact has been confirmed and documented by witnesses. It was then that the Kelly's realized that something extraordinary had occurred. A heavenly messenger had been sent as a sign and witness to the truth imparted from God's Word.

Fruitful Results

Naturally, these unusual signs and wonders do not occur needlessly. There must be some fruit or affirmation that is generated which advances God's kingdom. The Lord very often allows manifestations of His Spirit with signs and wonders as:

1. A witness to the messages presented and their present emphasis.
2. An encouragement to the faith of His people.
3. Mobilization of His body into His plan and into their destiny.
4. Spiritual awakening to the lost and lukewarm.

This was the fruit of the sign and wonder in Cincinnati.

Numerous witnesses have been interviewed on tape verifying their encounters with the messenger from God who took on the appearance of this brother as an affirmation of the spiritual realities being imparted during the conference. There has been a great surge of faith birthed in God's people as a result of this sign.

(More information and documentation on this occurrence can be obtained from David and Donna Kelly: http://passionandfire.org).

Entertaining Angels

This was quite an unusual occurrence but one that has been extensively scrutinized and validated. The Bible provides the only source of genuine affirmation of such an encounter. The Scripture admonishes us to:

Let love of the brethren continue.

Do not neglect to show hospitality to strangers, for by this some have entertained angels without knowing it (Hebrews 13:1-2).

The Bible records countless instances of angelic appearances that marked seasons of transition and advancement. This is especially true in the early apostolic church. There is an essential cooperation between heaven and earth.

We discover the Lord Jesus walking along the road to Emmaus in "another form" in the Gospel of Luke. The two disciples did not recognize Him until He came into their home and broke bread before them (see Luke 24).

In the book of Acts, we also notice Peter's supernatural deliverance from jail. As he came to the home of the disciples, the young girl who opened the door was startled to see who she perceived was Peter. Upon reporting this to the other disciples, they responded that it must have been his angel. This clearly implies that there were spiritual messengers working with them who took the form and appearance of the disciples.

This gospel of the kingdom was first declared by the Lord, evidenced by the Holy Spirit, and endorsed by God. He showed His approval of the gospel of power through signs and wonders and miraculous manifestations of the heavenly realm. Angelic appearances and supernatural signs awaken people from apathy and lethargy and re-ignite hearts that have grown cold or lukewarm.

God's Motivation

It is not my intent to overly emphasize signs and wonders, but rather the messages they convey. There must also be a genuine fruitfulness that comes from the manifestation of the Spirit. To more fully understand our mission and function on earth, we must also comprehend God's motivation. Our heavenly Father's desire is to display His glory and bring the full measure of His reward to His Son. This is accomplished through the preaching of His Word and the testimony of His power.

> **Angelic appearances and supernatural signs awaken people from apathy and lethargy and re-ignite hearts that have grown cold or lukewarm.**

When our motivations are firmly planted in the Lord's heart, then we are biblically justified when we long to see manifestations of His Spirit that glorify His name and convey salvation to the lost. The book of Acts alone records as many as seventeen instances of conversions birthed out of supernatural encounters.

Ultimately, our highest purpose is to delight in God and display the essence of who He is to a needy generation. We simply cannot accomplish this mandate in our own strength. We need His empowering Presence and the vindication of His Spirit. ◼

BORN FOR BATTLE

All Scriptures are New International Version unless otherwise indicated.

by Colin Brown

A line has been drawn! An epic spiritual battle is looming larger by the day. Those who know they have been born for battle have been summoned to fight the good fight. Arising is a corporate **"man after my own heart; he will do everything I want him to do" (Acts 13:22).**

Armed with the grace of God, a valiant and uncompromising new leadership is emerging—an army and family devoted to the Lord and truth. A common proclamation among their ranks echoes David's valor: **"For who is God besides the Lord? And who is the Rock except our God?" (Psalm 18:31)**

An acute awareness among them is that the kingdom of God is near. With boldness and humility, they are standing firm and moving in step with the Spirit. Wisdom guards their focus for they are mindful of their weaknesses, agreeing, **"But we have this treasure in jars of clay to show that this all-surpassing power is from God and not from us" (II Corinthians 4:7).**

Power Lines

An irrepressible force for advancing the kingdom of light is in the making. There are strategic and vital connections among the troops being put in place. These "power lines" are the result of sincere and heartfelt relational connections.

These powerful points of contact between the troops, while profound, usually occur with a quiet simplicity and little fanfare. To experience this work of the Spirit is to know the very real difference between the yoke the world places on us to make things happen as distinct from how Jesus does it. This yoke of the call to His service, as a call to battle, and to revive the battle weary, is: **"Walk with Me and work with Me—watch how I do it...Keep company with Me"** (Matthew 11:29-30 The Message).

No soldier of the Lord Jesus Christ is called to be isolated or out on his or her own. We are each remarkably interwoven together in our union with the Lord, as a tapestry of extraordinary handiwork. Each of us are enlisted as a vital part of a great family, army, and fellowship on earth, intimately related to the great company of witnesses and veterans in heaven, who have fought the good fight of faith before us.

This present greatest of movements among the troops ever to be witnessed is progressively gathering momentum and generating a synergy of the Spirit where: **"Five of you will chase a hundred, and a hundred of you will chase ten thousand, and your enemies will fall by the sword before you"** (Leviticus 26:8).

The Blessing of Strong Opposition

Opposition sharpens and defines us! Politically speaking, it has been said, "Strong opposition always leads to good government." This is true for the church where in the wisdom of God, a powerful and unrelenting enemy does us much good. Facing such opposition keeps us on our knees, on our toes, and on the edge of our seat in the very best sense.

We are being made to be **"dressed ready for service"** (Luke 12:35).

Developing the character of the Lord Jesus in the church through such tough spiritual warfare, even on our own soil, is integral to this calling in being born for battle. Remember that this fight is not against flesh and blood, and that the weapons of our warfare are not the weapons of this world (see Ephesians 6:10-18; II Corinthians 10:3-5).

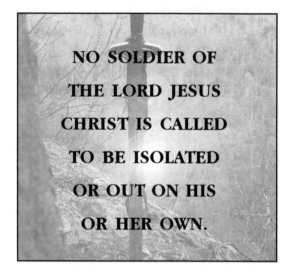

NO SOLDIER OF THE LORD JESUS CHRIST IS CALLED TO BE ISOLATED OR OUT ON HIS OR HER OWN.

Joseph's ability to govern with wisdom in Egypt was learned this way. In the face of fierce opposition, so very close to home, the true character of his heart was solicited to be strong. In summary of the tremendous conflict he endured, he nobly declared, **"You intended to harm me, but God intended it for good to accomplish what is now being done, the saving of many lives"** (Genesis 50:20).

Paul likewise sought to encourage his Corinthian friends, openly sharing the difficulties confronted on the battlefield of our calling, and the importance of prayer for each other, especially when the heat is on.

We do not want you to be uninformed, brothers, about the hardships we suffered in the province of Asia. We were under great pressure, far beyond our ability to endure, so that we despaired even of life.

Indeed, in our hearts we felt the sentence of death. But this happened that we might not rely on ourselves but on God, who raises the dead.

He has delivered us from such a deadly peril, and he will deliver us. On him we have set our hope that he will continue to deliver us,

as you help us by your prayers. Then many will give thanks on our behalf for the gracious favor granted us in answer to the prayers of many (II Corinthians 1:8-11).

RETREATING AS A RESULT OF FOCUSING ON OUR INADEQUACIES OR FAILURES IS NOT AN OPTION.

Faithfulness through thick and thin is a powerful and telling sign of the love of Christ having worked deeply in the hearts of the sons and daughters of the King.

These overcomers triumph through Him against the pride filled notions of another god. Like Habakkuk, they have received the revelation: **"See, he is puffed up; his desires are not upright—but the righteous will live by his faith"** (Habakkuk 2:4).

Retreating Is Not An Option!

Retreating as a result of focusing on our inadequacies or failures is not an option. Turning to the Lord is always and the only right thing to do. Faith is the resolute focus in the eyes of Abraham's offspring. **"Against all hope, Abraham in hope believed ...Without weakening in his faith, he faced the fact that his body was as good as dead...Yet he did not waver through unbelief regarding the promise of God, but was strengthened in his faith and gave glory to God, being fully persuaded that God had power to do what he had promised"** (Romans 4:18-21).

In this theater of great spiritual conflict, God's power is seen in the grace we are given to rise above the darkness and troubles of the hour. These include both inward and outward turmoil and troubles, like those that Job faced.

His very great and precious promises found in His Word, along with the grace of the prophetic that stands in keeping with the Scriptures, spur us on beyond the thought of ever retreating. **"And let us consider how we may spur one another on toward love and good deeds. Let us not give up meeting together, as some are in the habit of** doing, but encouraging one another—and all the more as you see the Day approaching" (Hebrews 10:24-25).

In Rick Joyner's book, *The Torch and The Sword*, an extraordinary and very wise young girl (see Chapter 3), emulates the character of Abraham's faith, in view of the battles she faces personally and otherwise. She imparts some great gems of wisdom, like: "They have us completely surrounded now. But anyone with courage to keep moving even when they are attacked can make it through their ranks...I was told that when they saw my resolve that they would give way before me, and they did."

In speaking lovingly, yet soberly about her mother, the young girl said, "She taught me very well, but she could not do what she taught me to do... When she hesitated and started to retreat she was quickly overcome. She then began ridiculing me with the rest of them. Once you begin to retreat before the evil ones, you are easy prey for them. She is now one of their prisoners...I could not let that stop me."

This young girl showed a wisdom that surpassed her mother's. How sobering that what our mouths declare that we wholeheartedly believe is only of real substance in how we live, especially in the theatre of battle. Our Christlike courage is most evident in the face of great difficulty and adversity. Be assured, what we say we believe will be thoroughly tested. Testing will surely come!

Even when those who are dearest to us stumble, our focus must remain primarily on the Rock. **"You will keep in** perfect peace him whose mind is steadfast, because he trusts in you. Trust in the Lord forever, for the Lord, the Lord, is the Rock eternal" (Isaiah 26:3-4).

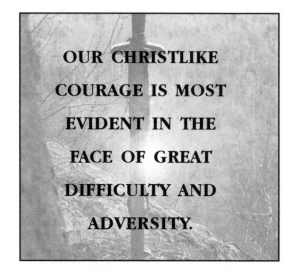

OUR CHRISTLIKE COURAGE IS MOST EVIDENT IN THE FACE OF GREAT DIFFICULTY AND ADVERSITY.

A Soldier's Prophetic Dream

The landscape of the church is completely changing! A very different outlook from what we have known will emerge. I came to understand this in a dream I had in October 2002, which helped me to appreciate what God is doing with His church, to conform us to the image of His Son.

I had gone to sleep very tired. I dreamed that I was riding with a good friend in his car. Eventually, we found ourselves at a beach that was very familiar to me because I had spent much time there when I was younger.

I got out of the car and walked toward an elevated view of the beachfront. Its landscape had changed significantly, and it was clear that a powerful storm had altered it.

As I stood there, I observed various types of heavy machinery on the sand. The workers were determined to recover the familiar old landscape to which they were so accustomed. I realized that this was a picture of how many in church are resistant to change, even while the Lord is reshaping the church as seems best to Him (see Jeremiah 18:1-6).

> THIS EXTRAORDINARY AND AWESOME WORK WAS AN ACT OF LOVE AND GREAT KINDNESS, AS WELL AS JUSTICE AND MERCY.

I was then shocked to see another storm in the form of a powerful, sandy whirlwind, bearing down upon these workers and their man-made devices. They had no knowledge of or sensitivity to the danger they were facing. Yet, even more gripping was the closeness and direction of many more of these powerful whirlwinds out of the sea that were headed straight for the beach. Beyond a shadow of a doubt, these winds of the Spirit again would totally and radically change the landscape of the beach.

As I stood there seeing what those on the beach could not, I was consumed with a profound sense of the fear of the Lord. This extraordinary and awesome work was an act of love and great kindness, as well as justice and mercy. The kingdom of heaven was at hand.

All the same, as much as I wanted to, I could not make those on the beach see that their efforts were working against the Lord's purposes. Nor could I alert them to the great danger they faced because of the noise of their machinery.

As I considered this insight after waking, I realized how much the fear of change makes for such resistant hearts, and seeks to incapacitate a new and fresh movement, even the movement of God. However, when the Lord is moving and recovering His domain as He is now doing, nothing can alter what He has decreed. A line has been drawn!

The wisdom of Gamaliel remains by addressing those who stand in opposition to the very One they think they defend. **"Leave these men alone! Let them go! For if their purpose or activity is of human origin, it will fail. But if it is from God, you will not be able to stop these men; you will only find yourselves fighting against God"** (Acts 5:38-39).

The Maturity of a Soldier's Character

Those who were born for battle and have an understanding of the times must focus their attention primarily on the Lord Himself, not their opposition, inwardly or outwardly. As one senior officer put it to a younger fellow soldier: **"Endure hardship with us like a good soldier of Christ Jesus. No one serving as a soldier gets involved in civilian affairs, he wants to please his commanding officer"** (II Timothy 2:3-4).

Rick Joyner has said, "Our first goal must be to confront and overcome our personal demons and our personal fears, so that we can grow in the authority to take on bigger demons and set other people free... We can win this war if we grow in faith. True faith...is the result of a living relationship with the God who loves us, has called us, and will empower us to do all that He created us to do" (*Breaking the Power of Evil*, pgs. 40-41).

The apprenticeship of faith and the maturity of the soldier's character of heart warrants more attention than most other matters and things. The real changes at hand are related to the condition and health of the human heart. Maturity is deeply connected to the wisdom that says, **"Above all else, guard your heart, for it is the wellspring of life"** (Proverbs 4:23).

Finishing Well

These are both exciting and sobering days. To have been born for battle at such a time as this is ranked among the highest of honors. How blessed we are! All the same, we are called to walk a narrow path indeed. Our personal and corporate vigilance is as crucial as David's, where our choices have eternal implications. Let us together, before the Lord, choose well!

"His (God's) **intent was that now, through the church, the manifold wisdom of God should be made known to the rulers and authorities in the heavenly realms,**

according to his eternal purpose which he accomplished

in Christ Jesus our Lord" (Ephesians 3:10-11).

For those born for battle, this unique day is an opportunity for embracing the worth and surpassing greatness of knowing Jesus our Lord, Savior, and Friend. What a privilege and honor to know the power of His resurrection and to participate in the fellowship of His sufferings, by becoming like Him in His death (see Philippians 3:7-11).

> **TO HAVE BEEN BORN FOR BATTLE AT SUCH A TIME AS THIS IS RANKED AMONG THE HIGHEST OF HONORS.**

Those who fight the good fight and finish well will see the glory of God revealed, the holiness of His Name restored, and the manifold wisdom of His ways exalted. With His fire and passion dwelling in our hearts, flowing forth as words of life, we will know this: **"'My name will be great among the nations, from the rising to the setting of the sun. In every place incense** (prayer) **and pure offerings** (expressions and gifts of sincere gratitude) **will be brought to my name, because my name will be great among the nations,' says the Lord Almighty"** (Malachi 1:11). ■

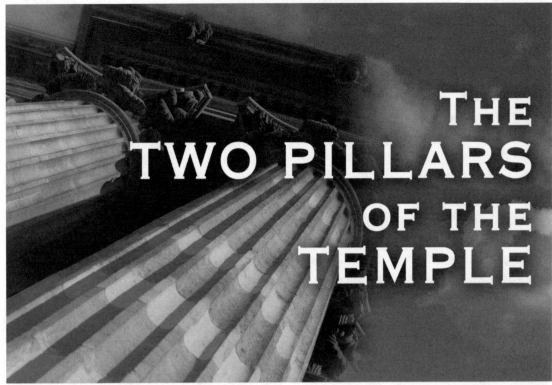

THE TWO PILLARS OF THE TEMPLE

by Rick Joyner

Thus he set up the pillars at the porch of the nave; and he set up the right pillar and named it Jachin, and he set up the left pillar and named it Boaz (I Kings 7:21).

Jachin was a priest and Boaz was a businessman (see I Chronicles 9:10, Nehemiah 11:10, Ruth 2:1). That these were chosen to be the two pillars of the temple is a prophetic statement that these are to be the two foundational ministries of the church, "the temple not made with hands." How can this be? Understanding this is crucial to understanding the church as it is intended to be. This is because the purpose of the ministry of the church is to reach people in everyday life. Business or commerce is the place of the most basic human transactions with one another, and this is where God wants to do some of His greatest works.

It is a false concept many have that most biblical heroes were priests, or those who we would see today as being in full-time ministry. The fact is that the overwhelming majority of the great men and women in Scripture were either farmers, businessmen, military men, or government officials, not priests. These include: Abraham, Isaac, Jacob, Joseph, Moses, Joshua, all of the judges, David, Daniel, Nehemiah, Esther, all but a couple of the prophets, all of the apostles when they were called, Cornelius, and almost all of the other ministries named in the New Testament.

Most of the great heroes of the faith in Scripture continued to work in their "secular profession" or trade the whole time they performed their work for the Lord. Even the great apostle Paul continued to make tents from time to time. He was not doing this as a hobby or because he needed the money, but to keep himself in touch with the practical issues of life that are essential if one is to have a truly relevant ministry. It is for this reason that the Lord will only entrust with the heavenly riches those who have been faithful with earthly riches (see Luke 16:11).

Also, this is the reason that some of the greatest heroes of the faith were also very wealthy and/or powerful, such as the patriarchs, Joseph, David, Daniel, and others. Without question, the pursuit of riches can be a major spiritual stumbling block, but when kept in their proper place, which means to use them properly for the kingdom as stewards who have been entrusted with them, learning to manage them properly can help us to be prepared for the **"true riches" (Luke 16:11).**

The fact remains true that almost any profession or trade seems to be the best platform for being launched into a life of extraordinary accomplishments in the Lord, just as the Lord Jesus Himself chose all of His own apostles from among the everyday trades and businesses of the time. These trades and businesses were their seminary, and it trained them up in such a way that they would never be out of touch with the common man.

The true temple of authentic Christianity is life itself. A factor in the coming great revolution of the church age will be when we break out of the prison of the modern concept of what church is. Church is not something we go to—it is our life and must be as real to us on Monday morning as it was on Sunday morning.

> **...the Lord will only entrust with the heavenly riches those who have been faithful with earthly riches.**

Though our times of corporate worship, teaching, and ministry are important, true church is 24 hours a day, 7 days a week. The services and church meetings are where we get much of our spiritual food and equipping for going to the frontline of the battle, daily life. Therefore, the Lord does not judge His church by how good the meetings are Sunday morning, but how good the people are doing Monday morning, Tuesday afternoon, and so on.

We should worship God as much Monday morning as we do Sunday morning. This does not mean that we need to sing choruses or hymns at work, but everything we do should be done as unto the Lord as worship to Him.

Consider this: It was said of many that the Holy Spirit came upon them, but who was the first one in Scripture to be *filled* with the Holy Spirit? We read about Him in Exodus 31:1-3:

> Now the LORD spoke to Moses, saying,
>
> "See, I have called by name Bezalel, the son of Uri, the son of Hur, of the tribe of Judah.
>
> And I have filled him with the Spirit of God in wisdom, in understanding, in knowledge, and in all kinds of craftsmanship.

We must start to see every job that we have as worship done for the Lord.

As Robert Frazier points out in his excellent book, *Marketplace Christianity,* Bezalel was not filled with the Holy Spirit for the purpose of miracles or prophecy, but for craftsmanship! Have you considered that your job, your skill, is holy to the Lord? Consider Colossians 3:23-24:

> Whatever you do, do your work heartily, as for the Lord rather than for men;
>
> knowing that from the Lord you will receive the reward of the inheritance. It is the Lord Christ whom you serve.

If we are doing our work for our boss, the corporation, or whoever else makes out our paycheck, then we are not living as we should, but have a thick veil over our eyes. If we work for men, then it will be from men that we receive our promotions and rewards. If we do our work as unto the Lord, then it is from Him that we will receive our rewards. Who would you rather work for? Who do you think can take care of you better?

We must start to see every job that we have as worship done for the Lord. Therefore, everything we do should be of the highest standards of excellence. We should have a vision of growing in our skills and the knowledge of our jobs so as to continually improve our performance. As Martin Luther King, Jr. once said, "If you are a street sweeper then sweep streets like Michelangelo painted!"

It should not matter to us if men give us credit for it or not, as we have a greater confidence that God will. This can bring a liberty and peace to our lives that helps us to overcome the stress and problems that many suffer in their jobs. Then we can focus on something even greater, helping to save the souls of those who work with us.

We need to see our jobs as "holy unto the Lord," and that He will even fill us with His Spirit for the purpose of excellence in our profession or trade. One of the greatest inspirations of my life was not a Christian, but he was considered one of the greatest pilots in the world. Every time he got in an airplane, he did so with the resolve to fly it better than he did the last time. He was an unrelenting perfectionist, and flying with him in the cockpit was one of the most intimidating jobs I have ever had. But he instilled in me a passion for excellence and to continually improve whatever I did, which I have honestly not seen in another Christian to that degree. This is a tragic irony. Certainly those who serve the King of kings should be this!

We should also learn how to use our spiritual gifts in our job. Some might consider it profane to use the gift of prophecy for helping us in our jobs, but the Lord wants to be involved in everything we do, and He also wants to prosper us in everything we do. Just as the Israelites in captivity were told to pray for the peace and prosperity of the nations to which they were scattered so that they would live in peace and enjoy prosperity, the Lord wants to use us as a blessing wherever we go. Isn't that what He did with Joseph, Daniel, and others? Did they not use their gifts in this way?

The prophetic gifts are especially useful in everyday life and can get the attention of many others quickly, just as a single word of knowledge about the woman at the well ended up stirring a whole city. Ask the Lord to give you words of knowledge, words of wisdom which is a supernatural wisdom, discernment of spirits, and prophecy for your job. Like

Joseph and Daniel, such can turn even the heart of the most powerful kings, which means they could certainly touch your boss.

When we do this we should also use the kind of discretion that the Lord Himself used with the woman at the well. He did not thunder "Thus saith the Lord!" at her. He gently let her know that He knew more about her, and she started asking the questions. We do not need or want the religious bombast that many seem to believe prophecy must come with. That is really more demeaning to the gift than helpful.

> The Lord wants to be involved in everything we do, and He also wants to prosper us in everything we do.

Of course, we need wisdom and discretion in how we use any gift of the Holy Spirit, always keeping in mind that He is holy. Do this, but also keep in mind that you are there as a Joseph or Daniel to help guide maybe even heathen leaders with the wisdom supplied by the Lord. This is not just to give you an edge in your job, though it certainly will do that, but it is to be a blessing and help to those the Lord has sent us to. As the Lord Himself explained in Matthew 5:43-45:

> "You have heard that it was said, 'You shall love your neighbor, and hate your enemy.'
>
> "But I say to you, love your enemies, and pray for those who persecute you
>
> in order that you may be sons of your Father who is in heaven; for He causes His sun to rise on the evil and the good, and sends rain on the righteous and the unrighteous.

Good management is one of the most essential needs and greatest lacks within the church.

The Lord was even willing to heal those who did not even return to thank Him. He will actually do many great miracles for people who will not even acknowledge Him or the miracles. Why? Because most of what He does He does just because He loves people and wants to help them. We are called to be a light to the world even though most of the world will reject it. He wants us to be a light to people even if they do not acknowledge it or give Him the glory for

His goodness. That is the nature of love, and God loves the whole world.

The Good Steward

Good management is essential for accomplishing anything of significance. Good management is one of the most essential needs and greatest lacks within the church. Anyone who is entrusted with anything of value, who does not develop good leadership and management skills for stewarding it, will either lose or bury their talents.

There is a great delusion that managers are born and not made. After nearly twenty-five years of studying leadership and management, I am convinced that some are born with either of these gifts, but also either can be acquired and developed. We may be born with the calling and gifts, but if we do not proactively develop them, they will decrease instead of mature.

Basic management skills and knowledge are the same whether they are applied to a business, a team, an army, or the church. Good pastors assess the people and resources they have been entrusted with and use them the most effectively for the kingdom. They also help equip their people to overcome in life, in all that they do, for the sake of the gospel.

As a pastor I feel that my greatest success will be to see every soul who I have been entrusted to help oversee stand before the Lord on that great day and hear **"Well done, good and faithful servant!" (Matthew 25:21** NIV**).** I therefore have to look at each person as a sacred trust, the Lord's own children who He entrusted me to watch over and equip for their purpose. I cannot possibly do this without using good management skills.

I oversee eight ministries, each of which I could devote all of my time to and not feel that it is enough. One day when I was feeling the pressure of this almost to the breaking point, I cried out to God. He immediately answered, "You know, I uphold the universe with My power. I can help you with this." Of course I knew the doctrine very well about how His yoke is easy and His burden light, the one that He gives to us is light, and even had some great teachings on them (see Matthew 11:30). But I was just not doing it in the very place where it is needed the most— the ministry to His church! It was because of this I started studying how He managed the universe, and I saw the glory of God in a way that radically changed my life.

Good management principles are essential for using the talents that He has entrusted to us for the maximum return for His kingdom. His good management principles are what uphold the universe, and it is a common grace that is available to all men, whether they acknowledge Him or not. They can be used for good or evil, but to date they are mostly used for evil. Instead of shying away from them because of this, we need to start using them for good! We do want to take the kingdom to the marketplace, and there is a lot from the marketplace that we do not want to bring back into the church.

However, there are some things we can learn from those who are successful in any field about management and leadership that the church desperately needs. Even though common grace is available to all men, it is still from God.

> **Good management principles are essential for using the talents that He has entrusted to us for the maximum return for His kingdom.**

It is for this reason that I require everyone on our leadership team to read at least two books a year on management and leadership. It does not matter how gifted one is, those who excel in any field, whether it is business, a trade, a sport, or even the military, are the ones who are continually reviewing and practicing the basics of their profession. They also seek to improve and further develop whatever gifts and skills they have been given.

In the Parable of the Talents, it was the slave who buried the talent that he was entrusted with which was called a "wicked, evil slave" (see Matthew 25:26). I think this is the last thing anyone should want to hear on that day when we must all stand before the judgment seat of Christ. The slaves in this parable who were told to **"enter into the joy of your master,"** **(Matthew 25:23)** were the ones who multiplied what they were entrusted with.

> **When the church fully matures it is going to be like Christ, doing the works that He did, like He did them, and where He did them.**

Now if all of the gifts and ministries of the Spirit were only to be used in church meetings, and if we truly equipped the saints to do the work of the ministry, where would they do this? It would not be possible for everyone to function in their gifts and ministries in just the few hours each week that are usually devoted to church meetings. Even with all of the home groups this is not possible. It is also essential we understand that the Lord does not want to be limited to just using us a few hours each week! The gifts and ministries we have been given are obviously to be used in everyday life.

I have come to believe that at least 85 percent of the gifts and ministries that have been entrusted to the church are not for use in our church services, but rather in everyday life. Isn't this where the Lord did the great majority of His own ministry? When the church fully matures it is going to be like Christ, doing the works that He did, like He did them, and where He did them.

Summary

We must understand how the two pillars of the temple are both the priestly ministry that we have all been given, and the ministry in business that we have also been given. Business is the place of basic human transactions, and God wants into all of them. These two pillars fit together, work together, and are both needed if the church is going to become what it is called to be. Billy Graham said, "I believe that one of the next great moves of God will be in the workplace." This is a true prophecy. We need to understand it and prepare for it.

This article is simply intended to stir you to hear the trumpet call that is being sounded almost universally now in the church about marketplace ministry. This is not a low calling. Ministry in the church, or what we now think of as church, is the high calling. The ministry in our church services is intended to feed, supply, train, and equip the soldiers who are on the frontline of the battle, which is the true ministry, which is everyday life. Until the very end of this age all but a few of the great men and women of faith, and the great exploits of the faith, will be found among these frontline soldiers of the kingdom. ∎

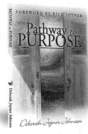

MORNINGSTAR | *School of Ministry*
Ephesians 4:1 Live Worthy of the Calling

MSM is a one or two year curriculum, depending on your needs and experience. Graduates of the first year curriculum can go on to an internship program with the MorningStar leadership team.

The MSM curriculum is intended to raise up a new generation of radical Christian leaders who are committed to sound biblical truth, to being like Christ, doing the works that He did, and never retreating before the enemies of the cross.

Housing available for 2005-2006 term.

MorningStar School of Ministry has been approved by the president of the University of North Carolina and the UNC Board of Governors to offer an Associate Degree in Christian Ministry.

For more information or to request an application call 803-547-9655 or write to MSM, P.O. Box 19409, Charlotte NC 28219

This school is authorized under Federal law to enroll non-immigrant students.

MorningStar on Television

The MorningStar Program can now be seen on

TBN Church Channel on Direct TV
Thursdays at 9:30 p.m., EST.
If you would like to receive the TBN Church Channel on cable,
please solicit your local cable company.

We can also be seen in Europe, the Middle East, and North Africa on
GOD Revival
Wednesdays at 00:30 a.m. • Saturdays at 11:30 a.m.
Sundays at 19:30 p.m.

GOD Channel
Sundays at 9:00 a.m. • Mondays at 3:30 a.m., 4:00 p.m., 9:00 p.m. •
Thursday at 1:00 a.m. (UK time)

The programs include live worship as well as speakers and teachers that
we feel have a present word for the church in our times.

MORNINGSTAR WEBSITE
www.morningstarministries.org

Word for the Week From Rick Joyner • Special Bulletins for Current Events • Online Store with Books and Music • Conference Information • Q&A with Rick Joyner • MorningStar School of Ministry Information • MorningStar Fellowships—Charlotte • Wilkesboro • Winston-Salem • Wilmington • MorningStar Subscriptions—Journal • Prophetic Bulletin • Message of the Month • Itineraries ... AND MUCH MORE

[Equipping the Saints for the Work of Ministry]

MorningStar
FELLOWSHIP CHURCH

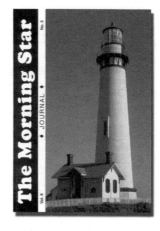

MorningStar Strategic Team

MST FINANCES

MST IS our partners' fellowship – those united with us in prayer and support of our strategic missions.

are invested in missions of strategic importance, such as the restoration of H.I.M. and the equipping and sending out of powerful and effective missions.

MEMBERS CONTRIBUTE

$15.00 per month, $150 per year, or more.

JOIN THE TEAM

Please send completed form to:
MorningStar, P.O. Box 440, Wilkesboro, NC 28697
Fax: 1-336-651-2430

Contact MST:
1-800-542-0278
mst@morningstarministries.org

Name _____ Date _____

Address _____

City _____ State _____ Zip _____

(_____)

Phone _____ E-mail _____

Here is my contribution of $_____ to MST in the form of:

☐ Cash ☐ Check ☐ Money Order (payable to MST) ☐ Credit Card

MSJ0605

Charge my:
☐ Master Card
☐ Visa
☐ Discover
☐ AMEX

Credit Card ☐☐☐☐ ☐☐☐☐ ☐☐☐☐ ☐☐☐☐   Expiration Date ☐☐/☐☐

Signature: _____ (Credit Card contributions will not be processed without a signature)

☐ Please automatically deduct $_____ from the above credit card each month.

Deducted the first business week of each month. Though we do not encourage debt, automatic deduction is a reliable method of supporting ministries conveniently. You may cancel at any time.

Note: MorningStar will never sell or give away your personal information. If for any reason you would like to stop deductions from your credit card or withdraw from MST, you can call 1-800-542-0278.

JOIN US IN A HISTORIC RESTORATION

MorningStar purchased the former Heritage USA Grand Hotel and Conference Center, along with fifty-two acres of property, and established Heritage International Ministries (H.I.M.).

HOTEL ROOM AT H.I.M.

THE NEHEMIAH PROJECT
RESTORE A HOTEL ROOM

You, your family, church, business, or group can restore a hotel room at H.I.M. Each room you help to restore will be named in your honor or as a memorial to the one you choose.

For more information, visit the H.I.M. section of www.morningstarministries.org. You can also contact Tiffany Taylor at HIM@morningstarministries.org or by calling 336-651-2400, ext. 113.

TAKE A SECTION OF THE WALL

Please send completed form to: The Nehemiah Project, P.O. Box 440, Wilkesboro, NC 28697

☐ **$5,000 to restore a hotel room**
For each $5,000 a room will be named in your honor. (You can pay installments of $500/month)

☐ **$1,000 or more**
For $1000 or more your name will be placed on our Nehemiah's wall. (You can pay installments of $100/month)

☐ **Any size donation**
Your name will be placed on the Permanent Register.

Name _____ Date _____

Address _____

City _____ State _____ Zip _____

(____) _____
Phone   E-mail

Here is my contribution of $_____ in the form of ☐ Cash ☐ Check ☐ Money Order ☐ CreditCard

Charge my:
☐ Master Card
☐ Visa
☐ Discover
☐ AMEX

Credit Card ☐☐☐☐ ☐☐☐☐ ☐☐☐☐ ☐☐☐☐

Expiration Date MSJ0605 ☐☐/☐☐

Signature: _____ (Credit Card contributions will not be processed without a signature)

☐ Please automatically deduct $_____ from the above credit card each month.
Deducted the first business week of each month. Though we do not encourage debt, automatic deduction is a reliable method of supporting ministries conveniently. You may cancel at any time.

Note: MorningStar will never sell or give away your personal information. If for any reason you would like to stop deductions from your credit card, please call 1-800-542-0278.

Statement of Ownership, Management, and Circulation
(Required by 39 U.S.C. 3685)

1. Publication Title: The Morning Star Journal® 2. Publication No.: 0129-03
3. Filing Date: October 1, 2005　　　　　4. Issue frequency: Quarterly
5. No. of issues published annually: 4　　6. Annual Subscription Price: $16.95 U.S.; $24.95 Int'l
7. Complete Mailing Address of Known Office of Publication: 1605 Industrial Drive., Wilkesboro, NC 28697
   Contact person: David Hart, Telephone: 336-651-2400, ext. 105
8. Complete Mailing Address of General Office of Publisher: same as #7
9. Publisher: MorningStar Publications, P.O. Box 440, Wilkesboro, NC 28697
   Editor: Rick Joyner, P.O. Box 440, Wilkesboro, NC 28697
   Managing Editor: Deborah Joyner Johnson, P.O. Box 440, Wilkesboro, NC 28697
10. Owner: MorningStar Fellowship Church, P.O. Box 440, Wilkesboro, NC 28697
11. There are no Bondholders, Mortgagees, or Other Security Holders.
12. The purpose, function, and nonprofit status of this organization and the exempt status for federal income tax purposes has not changed during the preceding 12 months.
13. Publication Title: The Morning Star Journal®
14. Issue Date of Circulation Date Below: October 2005
15. Extent and Nature of Circulation

	Average No. Copies Each Issue During Preceding 12 Months	No. Copies of Single Issue Published Nearest to Filing Date
a. Total No. of Copies (Net Press Run)	15,000	15,000
b. Paid and/or Requested Circulation		
(1)Paid/Requested Outside-County Mail Subscriptions	10,203	10,007
(2)Paid In-County Subscriptions	20	27
(3)Sales Through Dealers and Carriers, Street Vendors, and Counter Sales, and Other Non-USPS Paid Distribution	98	85
(4)Other Classes Mailed Through the USPS00		
c. Total Paid and/or Requested Circulation	10,321	10,119
d. Free Distribution by Mail		
(1) Outside-County	0	0
(2) In-County	0	0
(3) Other Classes Mailed Through the USPS	0	0
e. Free Distribution Outside the Mail	77	77
f. Total Free Distribution	77	77
g. Total Distribution	10,398	10,196
h. Copies Not Distributed	4,602	4,804
i. Total Sum of 15g. and h.)	15,000	15,000
j. Percent Paid and/or Requested Circulation	68%	67%

16. This Statement of Ownership will be printed in the Vol.15-4 issue of this publication.
David Hart, Office Business Manager, August 4, 2005